ARMAGEDDON APPROACHING

UNCOVER THE HOPEFUL
TRUTH ABOUT END-TIMES
BIBLICAL PROPHECY

David Cooper

Chosen
a division of Baker Pu...
Minneapolis, M...

© 2025 by David C. Cooper

Published by Chosen Books
Minneapolis, Minnesota
ChosenBooks.com

Chosen Books is a division of
Baker Publishing Group, Grand Rapids, Michigan

Printed in the United States of America

All rights reserved. No part of this publication may be reproduced, stored in a retrieval system, or transmitted in any form or by any means—for example, electronic, photocopy, recording—without the prior written permission of the publisher. The only exception is brief quotations in printed reviews.

Library of Congress Cataloging-in-Publication Data
Names: Cooper, David, 1956– author.
Title: Armageddon approaching : uncover the hopeful truth about end-times biblical prophecy / David Cooper.
Description: Minneapolis, Minnesota : Chosen Books, a division of Baker Publishing Group, [2025] | Includes bibliographical references.
Identifiers: LCCN 2024044743 | ISBN 9780800773250 (paperback) | ISBN 9780800773274 (casebound) | ISBN 9781493450930 (ebook)
Subjects: LCSH: Armageddon—Biblical teaching. | End of the world—Biblical teaching. | Bible—Prophecies—End of the world.
Classification: LCC BS649.A68 C66 2025 | DDC 236/.9—dc23/eng/20250215
LC record available at https://lccn.loc.gov/2024044743

Unless otherwise indicated, Scriptures taken from the Holy Bible, New International Version®, NIV®. Copyright © 1973, 1978, 1984, 2011 by Biblica, Inc.® Used by permission of Zondervan. All rights reserved worldwide. www.zondervan.com. The "NIV" and "New International Version" are trademarks registered in the United States Patent and Trademark Office by Biblica, Inc.®

Scripture quotations identified GNT are from the Good News Translation in Today's English Version-Second Edition. Copyright © 1992 by American Bible Society. Used by permission.

Scripture quotations identified KJV are from the King James Version of the Bible.

Scripture identified NKJV taken from the New King James Version®. Copyright © 1982 by Thomas Nelson. Used by permission. All rights reserved.

Scriptures identified NIV1984 taken from the Holy Bible, New International Version®, NIV®. Copyright © 1973, 1978, 1984 by Biblica, Inc.® Used by permission of Zondervan. All rights reserved worldwide. www.zondervan.com. The "NIV" and "New International Version" are trademarks registered in the United States Patent and Trademark Office by Biblica, Inc.®

Cover design by InsideOut Creative Arts, Inc.

Baker Publishing Group publications use paper produced from sustainable forestry practices and postconsumer waste whenever possible.

25 26 27 28 29 30 31   7 6 5 4 3 2 1

"That history and geopolitics are plunging toward some kind of finish line is hardly even controversial. The question is how? When? What will it mean for believers and nonbelievers? I heartily recommend Dr. David Cooper's newest book, *Armageddon Approaching*. Avoiding both shrill hysteria and smug academics, Dr. Cooper's book is timely, readable, and important."

Dr. Mark Rutland, executive director, National Institute of Christian Leadership

"For Christians and others seeking guidance about the end times, my friend Dr. David Cooper's book is indispensable. *Armageddon Approaching* faithfully adheres to biblical truth and is a welcome antidote to fear and falsehood. Dr. Cooper conveys the good news that God holds the world and humanity in His hands, and the final chapter ends with victory and eternity in the presence of Jesus Christ. I highly recommend this book for anyone else seeking to separate fact from fiction when it comes to the future. A must-read!"

Dr. Ralph Reed, founder and chairman, Faith & Freedom Coalition

"Out of the dark abyss of uncertainty, my friend Dr. David Cooper offers a bright spark of hope that the believer can stand firm on the conviction that Bible prophecy was meant to stir faith in God's promises. God is still in control and will return for His Church in His own time. A timely and encouraging manuscript."

Dr. R. C. Hugh Nelson, lead pastor, Ebenezer Urban Ministry Center, Brooklyn, New York

ARMAGEDDON APPROACHING

To my lovely wife, Barbie,
without whom I could not fulfill
God's purpose for my life to preach
the unreachable riches of Christ.

CONTENTS

Foreword by Jentezen Franklin 11
Introduction 13

1. Prophetic Signs 15
2. Future Shock 35
3. Israel Under Siege 51
4. The Days of Noah Return 63
5. The Society of Sodom 81
6. The Coming Global Order 99
7. Antichrist Arising 119
8. The Power behind the Throne 131
9. The War to End All Wars 153
10. Global Warming 167
11. The Government of God 183
12. A Skeptic's Guide to Faith 197

Acknowledgments 215
Notes 217

FOREWORD

The days we are living in are unprecedented as we watch biblical prophecy unfold right in front of our eyes. I cannot remember a time when so many pastors and Bible scholars all agree that we are on the precipice of what the Bible refers to as the "end times."

When it comes to Bible prophecy, I do not know of a teacher who can lay it out in practical and understandable language better than Dr. David Cooper. For decades he has been one of the leading authorities, both nationally and globally, for all things doctrinal and theological, not only for those he has pastored but for thousands upon thousands of those who have followed him over the years. He is a pastor and teacher you can learn from and grow under, and he has been a trusted friend to me personally.

In *Armageddon Approaching*, Dr. Cooper not only lays out the biblical timelines and events of the last days but does so in a way that brings hope, not condemnation; peace, not panic. The book reads like the evening news: prophetic signs, Israel under siege, the days of Noah returning, the coming

Foreword

global order, even the global warming controversy. These are the topics that all of us, both pastor and parishioner, wrestle with today. Chapter after chapter is filled with biblical facts couched in clear scriptural progression, bringing together the prophecies from a number of books of the Bible that discuss the end times.

It is no overstatement to say that every Bible-believing pastor in every pulpit and classroom around the world is called to stand and proclaim that the end is near and then to teach what God's Word has to say about end-times prophecy. It is irresponsible to preach week in and week out and not warn people that the Lord could return any day or even any minute. The message is imperative all through the Old and New Testament to "get ready."

Armageddon Approaching will walk you through every aspect of end-times theology in a way that both scholars and the average man or woman in the pew can understand and apply to their lives.

Jentezen Franklin, senior pastor,
Free Chapel, Gainesville, Georgia

INTRODUCTION

A friend once told the American humorist Mark Twain, "I'm worried. The world is coming to an end."

"Don't worry about the world," he replied. "We can get along without it."[1]

While people have many personal worries in common, such as financial stability, healthcare, and family concerns, global worries loom large. The media bombards us 24/7 with distressing and frightening stories and images of world problems. We live in a state of chronic worry about the world at large.

An article entitled "What Worries the World" provides a snapshot of world opinion on global issues. Inflation remains the number one issue for the past twenty-five months, followed by such concerns as poverty and social inequality, crime and violence, military conflict among nations, healthcare, immigration, moral decline, terrorism, environmental threats, and maintaining social programs.[2] Such global fears echo the prophecy of Jesus concerning the last days: "People

Introduction

will faint from terror, apprehensive of what is coming on the world, for the heavenly bodies will be shaken" (Luke 21:26).

But the Bible assures us that the world lies safely in the hands of God. Its future destiny is not termination but transformation when God ushers in a new heaven and a new earth. The final chapter of human history will be written when Jesus Christ returns as King of kings and Lord of lords. The New Testament contains 318 references to His return. The Bible is the index of the future and tells us that God remains in control and that Christ will return.

While many books on end-times prophecy focus on speculation and sensationalism, we will focus our attention not on the things shrouded in mystery but on what God has revealed. Jesus said, "It is not for you to know the times or dates that the Father has set by his own authority" (Acts 1:7). The word *set* means predestined. The destiny of the world is predestined by God.

Jesus went on to call the Church to focus on her mission today and not worry about the future, which belongs to God. He instructed His disciples (and us): "But you will receive power when the Holy Spirit comes on you; and you will be my witnesses . . . to the ends of the earth" (Acts 1:8).

While the world is gripped with fear, we know that the future is as bright as the promises of God. As God's people, we are "looking for the blessed hope and glorious appearing of our great God and Savior Jesus Christ" (Titus 2:13 NKJV).

As you read this book, may you gain understanding of simple yet profound truths about Bible prophecy and find hope in God's promise of our fantastic future of faith.

ONE

PROPHETIC SIGNS

When I was in elementary school, I struggled with learning to tell time. I got the big hand and the little hand confused. I thought the big hand should stand for hours and the little hand for minutes. An hour is bigger than a minute, I thought, so it should get the big hand. I stayed after school every day for a week while my teacher spent time to teach me how to tell time.

While nearly everyone can tell time in the natural realm, not everyone can tell time spiritually. Jesus said we need to be able to discern the signs of the times. The Pharisees and Sadducees came to Jesus and tested Him by asking Him to show them a sign from heaven. He replied:

> "When evening comes, you say, 'It will be fair weather, for the sky is red,' and in the morning, 'Today it will be stormy, for the sky is red and overcast.' You know how to interpret the appearance of the sky, but *you cannot interpret the signs of the times*."
>
> Matthew 16:2–3, emphasis added

What is a spiritual sign? The prophet Isaiah said that he and his sons were signs and symbols: "Here am I, and the children the LORD has given me. We are signs and symbols in Israel from the LORD Almighty, who dwells on Mount Zion" (Isaiah 8:18). They were signs of hope that God was doing a new thing.

When the angel appeared to the shepherds in Bethlehem and announced the Savior's birth, he told them, "This will be a sign to you: You will find a baby wrapped in cloths and lying in a manger" (Luke 2:12). If Jesus had been born in a hotel, they would not have known where to find Him, because a hotel would have been full of people. But the manger was a feeding trough for animals in a stable, and there was only one baby in a stable, so it was easy to find Him. God used the stable as a sign for the shepherds to know where to go to see the Savior.

The writer of Hebrews tells us that God sends signs to confirm the Gospel of Christ: "God also testified to it by signs, wonders and various miracles, and by gifts of the Holy Spirit distributed according to his will" (Hebrews 2:4). Some say spiritual gifts ended with the apostles' ministry, but that is the furthest thing from the truth. God uses signs and wonders to reveal His power and confirm the Gospel.

Jesus said that in the last days,

"There will be signs in the sun, moon and stars. On the earth, nations will be in anguish and perplexity at the roaring and tossing of the sea. People will faint from terror, apprehensive of what is coming on the world, for the heavenly bodies will be shaken. At that time they will see the Son of Man coming in a cloud with power and great glory. When these things begin to take place, stand up and lift up your heads, because your redemption is drawing near."

Luke 21:25–28

A sign is an emblem or event given by God to announce a special occasion, to warn of danger, or to give us directions. We see signs on billboards, text messages, and emails about holiday sales. We see warning signs for bad weather, traffic jams, or dangerous construction zones. We follow road signs to slow down, to take a detour, or to take the next exit off the interstate.

Jesus told the religious leaders of His day that they could interpret the signs of the weather but could not see God at work in the world. He wept over Jerusalem at the end of His ministry and lamented, "You did not know the time of your visitation" (Luke 19:44 NIV).

While visiting Germany for a ministry opportunity, a friend and I rented a car to drive on the autobahn. The autobahn has no speed limit for 70 percent of its roadway, and I have always wanted to drive on it. The average speed is 90 mph. When we got on the autobahn, I floored it and never let up. The car maxed out at 140 mph! Even so, Mercedes, Audis, and Lamborghinis were passing me as if I were standing still. We saw road signs but had no idea what they meant because they were written in German. Then we saw a large sign that seemed to be a caution sign, but we did not know what it meant either. Suddenly the road narrowed to a single lane, and I braked quickly. I told my friend, "Apparently that sign read, *Slow Down!*"

What are the signs of the times telling us about the future? While many are anxious, those who know what the Bible teaches about the future anticipate the new world God is preparing. "'What no eye has seen, what no ear has heard, and what no human mind has conceived'—the things God has prepared for those who love him—these are the things God has revealed to us by his Spirit" (1 Corinthians 2:9–10).

Research shows that more than half of all Americans believe in the return of Jesus Christ; that the Antichrist will appear; and that the battle of Armageddon will occur. Armageddon is the final war as foretold in Scripture, when the Antichrist marches on Israel to destroy her and to control the world. Then Christ will return in power to defeat the Antichrist and establish the Kingdom of God on earth—the Kingdom that will never end.

The good news is that the end of this age is the beginning of a new age as God unfolds His eternal plan for the world. The signs of Jesus' return are all around us, reminding us that in God's perfect time, we will "see the Son of Man coming on the clouds of heaven, with power and great glory" (Matthew 24:30).

Curious Minds

Jesus' disciples were interested in the future, just as we are. And when Jesus predicted the destruction of the Temple, they asked Him three important questions: When will these things happen? What will be the sign of Your coming? And what will be the sign of the end of the age?

> Jesus answered: "Watch out that no one deceives you. For many will come in my name, claiming, 'I am the Messiah,' and will deceive many. You will hear of wars and rumors of wars, but see to it that you are not alarmed. Such things must happen, but the end is still to come. Nation will rise

Prophetic Signs

against nation, and kingdom against kingdom. There will be famines and earthquakes in various places. All these are the beginning of birth pains.

"Then you will be handed over to be persecuted and put to death, and you will be hated by all nations because of me. At that time many will turn away from the faith and will betray and hate each other, and many false prophets will appear and deceive many people. Because of the increase of wickedness, the love of most will grow cold, but the one who stands firm to the end will be saved. And this gospel of the kingdom will be preached in the whole world as a testimony to all nations, and then the end will come."

Matthew 24:4–14

Let's examine each of the three questions the disciples asked Jesus.

1. When Will These Things Happen?

Jesus' prophecy of the destruction of the Temple was fulfilled in AD 70.

The Temple sat on the summit of Mount Zion, on a plateau of one thousand square feet, and was built of white marble plated with gold. When the sun glistened on it, one could hardly look at it for its brilliance. It was surrounded by great porches, Solomon's Porch and the Royal Porch, supported by columns cut out of solid blocks of marble, each standing 37½ feet high. At each corner of the Temple stood stones measuring twenty to forty feet in length and weighing more than a hundred tons. How the stones were cut and placed in position remains a mystery of ancient engineering.

The war with Rome started in AD 66, when the Jewish people revolted against Rome two years after that city's great fire. The war lasted four years. The Romans suffered heavy casualties toward the end of the war, trying to lay siege to Jerusalem. Jewish forces put up a strong defense. Finally Titus, the Roman general, gave orders to set fire to the city gates. Soon the fire spread to the Temple, the last remaining sanctuary for Jewish soldiers.

The Romans drove the Jews back as far as the Temple itself, which the Jews were using as a citadel. One Roman soldier lifted another on his shoulders, who set fire to a golden window, through which a passage led to the rooms on the north side of the Temple. The Temple was now engulfed in flames. Titus, determined to save the sanctuary, ordered the soldiers to put out the fire, but their efforts were in vain. Like Pompey a century before, Titus stood in the Holy of Holies and was awed at what he saw.

That day was around the tenth of the month of Av, corresponding to August. (Many dates in history are approximate, especially when correlating the ancient Jewish calendar with the Gregorian calendar.) The first Temple had been destroyed on the same day, or near it, by Nebuchadnezzar, king of Babylon (see Jeremiah 52:12). Some ten thousand people died, and the Temple was disassembled without one stone left upon another, fulfilling Jesus' prophecy of its destruction. The Jewish people commemorate this tragedy on the ninth day of Av to honor those who died.[1]

2. What Will Be the Sign of Your Coming?

The second question referred to Jesus' coming as Messiah King to establish His Kingdom, as the Old Testament prophets had predicted. The disciples thought Jesus would bring the Kingdom by military and political force, leading a rebellion against Rome, but Jesus came into the world to establish the Kingdom of God in human hearts by giving us eternal life.

"The kingdom of God is within you," Jesus said (Luke 17:21 NKJV). When we are born again through faith in Him, we enter the Kingdom of God, and His Kingdom rules in our hearts. Jesus said, "No one can see the kingdom of God unless they are born again" (John 3:3).

3. What Will Be the Sign of the End of the Age?

The Old Testament prophets described history in two ages: the present age of sin and suffering and the age to come of righteousness and peace. For example, Isaiah wrote of the Messiah, "Of the greatness of his government and peace there will be no end" (Isaiah 9:7). This third question of the disciples, then, referred to the Messianic age.

Jesus will be exalted "far above all rule and authority, power and dominion, and every name that is invoked, not only in the present age but also in the one to come" (Ephesians 1:21). When we receive Christ as Savior, we have "tasted the goodness of the word of God and the powers of the coming age" (Hebrews 6:5). The day of the Lord is the world-changing event between the two ages, causing the first age to pass away and giving rise to the new age. The day of the Lord refers to the return of Christ.

What will happen in the last days? The greatest prophecies of the New Testament concern the Lord's return. The Old Testament contains 300 prophecies about Jesus' first coming as Savior, while the New Testament has 318 prophecies of His Second Coming as Lord. About one out of every twenty-five verses in the New Testament deals with Christ's return. That is how predominant the subject is in the Bible.

Jesus will rapture His people out of this world. The word *rapture* comes from the Latin translation of the Bible and means "to snatch away suddenly." The Rapture will be a sign to the world that the end of the age is at hand. We do not know exactly how this will happen—only that, according to the Bible, Jesus will take us out of this world and into eternity. He said, "If I go and prepare a place for you, I will come back and take you to be with me that you also may be where I am. You know the way to the place where I am going" (John 14:3–4). The place Jesus is preparing is heaven.

The Great Tribulation will take place over seven years, while the Antichrist rises to power. After he invades Jerusalem at the end of the Tribulation, he will be destroyed at the battle of Armageddon, when Jesus returns as "King of kings and Lord of lords" (Revelation 19:16). Then Jesus will set up His Kingdom on earth and govern the world in righteousness. This is "the coming age" (Hebrews 6:5), or the Millennium, meaning a thousand years (see Revelation 20:2). The Millennium will end with the final judgment and the destruction of Satan and evil (see Revelation 20:11–15). Then God will make "a new heaven and a new earth, where righteousness dwells" (2 Peter 3:13).

Jesus offered prophetic signs of His return to give us confidence in a world of confusion. The signs tell us that our God is in control of the movement and destiny of the history of the world. Don't focus on politics or worldwide problems, and don't panic. Rather, focus your faith on the prophetic promise that Jesus is coming again.

The future belongs to God, and you belong to God, so Jesus tells us, "When these things begin to take place, stand up and lift up your heads, because your redemption is drawing near" (Luke 21:28). Jesus gave clear signs of His return. We need to discern the times so we are ready.

The end of this age is the beginning of God's new world order under Jesus our King. When His Kingdom comes, the kingdoms of this earth will be no more.

The Prophetic Signs

Now that we have examined the disciples' three questions, let's look closely at the prophetic signs Jesus gave them. When He described the signs, He said, "But see to it that you are not alarmed. Such things must happen, but the end is still to come" (Matthew 24:6). Prophecy is given to alleviate our anxiety, not to cause us panic. When the world panics, we are at peace.

What were the prophetic signs Jesus gave?

The Sign of False Prophets and False Christs

This was the most frequent sign Jesus gave of the last days:

"Many false prophets will appear and deceive many people. . . . For false messiahs and false prophets will appear and perform great signs and wonders to deceive, if possible, even the elect. See, I have told you ahead of time."

Matthew 24:11, 24–25

So we must guard against spiritual deception. Paul warned, "The Spirit clearly says that in later times some will abandon the faith and follow deceiving spirits and things taught by demons" (1 Timothy 4:1). Don't get caught up in false spirituality and other religions. "Follow me," Jesus said— and nothing else or no one else. When you follow Jesus with single-minded loyalty, and base your beliefs only on the Bible, you will protect yourself from being misled spiritually.

The spirit of antichrist is already at work in the world to prepare the way for the Antichrist and his government (see 1 John 4:3). The apostle Paul explained:

> The time will come when people will not put up with sound doctrine. Instead, to suit their own desires, they will gather around them a great number of teachers to say what their itching ears want to hear. They will turn their ears away from the truth and turn aside to myths.
>
> 2 Timothy 4:3–4

So stand firm in your faith and don't be misled by myths.

The Sign of World Chaos

While the world has always experienced chaos, the last days will see chaotic conditions on a global level. Jesus said, "Nation will rise against nation, and kingdom against kingdom. There will be great earthquakes, famines and pestilences in various places, and fearful events and great signs from heaven" (Luke 21:10–11).

The coronavirus pandemic is an example of Jesus' prophecy about "pestilences in various places." The Greek word used for *pestilences* means plagues or diseases. What is different between the coronavirus pandemic and other viruses? The difference is that the coronavirus was more severe, and it was global, not local. It was the first time a virus shut down the entire world, stopped global travel, closed schools and churches, and shut national borders. The last days prophetic signs are global in scale and point to Christ's return.

Prophetic Signs

Is all this upheaval the direct judgment of God or the result of human sin? The answer is both. God's judgment is often the direct consequence of our sin. Sometimes God reaches down His hand from heaven with acts of judgment to discipline us and bring us to repentance and faith. The last days are a time of both judgment and salvation.

The book of Revelation depicts the coming judgment during the Great Tribulation with symbols—the seven trumpets and seven bowls of wrath. We read these sobering words: "Go, pour out the seven bowls of God's wrath on the earth" (Revelation 16:1). Suffering often results from the evil of war. Scientists tell us that if one hydrogen bomb, encased in cobalt, were detonated over the North Pole, it would kill every living creature in the whole Northern Hemisphere of this planet. Three billion people plus!

The Sign of Persecution

The early Church suffered greatly under Rome. Even today Christians in Communist and Islamic nations around the world suffer economic oppression, religious limitations, persecution, imprisonment, and even death. John the Revelator saw a vision of the martyrs crying for justice:

> When [the Lamb] opened the fifth seal, I saw under the altar the souls of those who had been slain because of the word of God and the testimony they had maintained. They called out in a loud voice, "How long, Sovereign Lord, holy and true, until you judge the inhabitants of the earth and avenge our blood?" Then each of them was given a white robe, and they were told to wait a little longer, until the full number of their fellow servants, their brothers and sisters, were killed just as they had been.
>
> Revelation 6:9–11

I saw an online news report one Sunday afternoon, after arriving home from a great worship service, when I opened my computer. The Islamic State had released a video purporting to show the beheadings of a group of Egyptian Christians kidnaped in Libya. Twenty-one Christians had been forced to their knees, then beheaded by ISIS. This terrorist organization threatened Christians, calling them "the people of the cross."[2]

While persecution is real and tragic, it is no threat to the Gospel of Christ and to faithful believers who stand firm to the end.

A pastor in India told me about a high government official who started a personal campaign to drive all the Christians out of India. He visited several cities and began to build a consensus among leaders for his cause. Then his daughter confessed to him that she had become a Christian. "If you drive all the Christians out of India," she told him, "you will drive me out of our home." He did not want to lose his daughter, so he stopped his persecution against believers.

I met a pastor from Pakistan who had fled the country because of persecution. His life was threatened, and he and his family had suffered greatly. When he fled the country, all his possessions were seized by the government, and he and his family were left destitute. Yet he stands firm in his faith in Christ and continues to preach the Gospel.

Persecution for Jesus' name is a privilege. When the apostles first began to suffer, they did not renounce their faith or stop telling others about Christ, as they were told to do. Instead,

The apostles left the Sanhedrin, rejoicing because they had been counted worthy of suffering disgrace for the Name.

Prophetic Signs

Day after day, in the temple courts and from house to house, they never stopped teaching and proclaiming the good news that Jesus is the Messiah.

Acts 5:41–42

The apostle Peter exhorted the suffering Church under the tyranny of Rome to stand firm in the faith:

Rejoice inasmuch as you participate in the sufferings of Christ, so that you may be overjoyed when his glory is revealed. If you are insulted because of the name of Christ, you are blessed, for the Spirit of glory and of God rests on you. If you suffer, it should not be as a murderer or thief or any other kind of criminal, or even as a meddler. However, if you suffer as a Christian, do not be ashamed, but praise God that you bear that name.

1 Peter 4:13–16

Here is one of only three places where the term *Christian* appears in the Bible. A true Christian is one who stands firm in the faith. We never give in to pressure. We never run out of resources. We never give up in discouragement. Persecution may be mild—being ridiculed or insulted for our faith—or as severe as martyrdom, as believers have experienced around the world. Regardless, we praise God that we bear the name *Christian*.

The Sign of Spiritual Weakness

Jesus said, "Because of the increase of wickedness, the love of most will grow cold" (Matthew 24:12). Some people will fall away from their faith in Jesus, especially those who believe casually in Jesus but have not committed their lives to Him. The last days will be a time when moral uncleanness will increase. Even in this day of moral relativism, immorality ridicules and utterly rejects biblical truth. Yet we stand faithful to Jesus and to the Word of God as a witness to the world that hope and eternal life are found in Christ.

Because of increased sinfulness in the last days, Jesus said, "the love of most will grow cold." He meant love for Him, as He told the Ephesian church: "You have left your first love" (Revelation 2:4 NKJV). Paul wrote that in the last days, "Some will abandon the faith" (1 Timothy 4:1). And he told his spiritual son Timothy that Demas, another of his fellow ministers, had left him "because he loved this world" (2 Timothy 4:10). Jesus asked, "When the Son of Man comes, will he find faith on the earth?" (Luke 18:8).

We answer enthusiastically, *Yes!* When Jesus returns, may He find faith in His people.

The last days will be a time when God sifts the wheat from the chaff. Jesus said, "The harvest is the end of the age. . . . The Son of Man will send out his angels, and they will weed out of his kingdom everything that causes sin and all who do evil" (Matthew 13:39, 41). The harvesting angels will separate the faithful from the unfaithful. Jesus will purge out of the ranks those "having a form of godliness but denying its power" (2 Timothy 3:5). Don't be a casual observer of Christianity—be a committed overcomer!

What are we to do as the world gets more sinful? Jesus gave us one of the most important challenges of discipleship: "The one who stands firm to the end will be saved" (Matthew 24:13). There is a cost to following Jesus. Paul referred to his imprisonment as sharing in the sufferings of Christ: "It has been granted to you on behalf of Christ not only to believe in him, but also to suffer for him" (Philippians 1:29). We need to stand up proudly to bear the name of Jesus. We follow in the footsteps of the One who laid down His life for our salvation, who prayed for His executioners, "Father, forgive them," and who taught us to love our enemies. We don't follow a leader or faith that advocates violence, that calls for jihad, or that persecutes those who do not believe as we do.

When false Christs and false prophets appear—stand! When we hear about wars and rumors of war—stand! When nation rises against nation and kingdom against kingdom—stand! When we learn of famines and earthquakes in many places—stand! When we are handed over to be persecuted and are hated by all nations for His name—stand! When many turn away from the faith—stand! When iniquity increases and the love of many toward God and toward Christ grows cold—stand!

Stand firm—you are the salt of the earth.

Stand firm—you are the light of the world.

Stand firm—you are a city set on a hill.

Stand firm—you are a chosen generation.

Stand firm—you are a royal priesthood.

Stand firm—you are a holy nation.

Stand firm—you are the people belonging to God.

Stand firm and "declare the praises of him who called you out of darkness into his wonderful light" (1 Peter 2:9).

The Sign of Global Missions

Jesus ended with a promising prophetic sign that we are seeing fulfilled today: "This gospel of the kingdom will be preached in the whole world as a testimony to all nations, and then the end will come" (Matthew 24:14). The good news of Jesus is being proclaimed around the world through global media.

Every week I preach to thousands of the faithful people of my church in Atlanta. Our media ministry broadcasts the sermon to thousands of worshipers all over the world. Those viewers then take the sermons and share them with others. They watch them online in house-based churches and organize Bible studies using my media-based messages. One sermon gets reproduced and shared over and over. Truly the Gospel of the Kingdom is being preached in the whole world! Global satellites are like angelic messengers proclaiming the Word of God to the world. Isaiah declared prophetically that "the earth will be filled with the knowledge of the LORD as the waters cover the sea" (Isaiah 11:9).

Early in my pastoral ministry, I concluded a sermon at Christmas by explaining that Jesus is revealed in every book of the Bible, from Genesis to Revelation. In Genesis Jesus is the seed of woman. In Exodus He is the Passover Lamb. And on through the Bible, until in Revelation Jesus is King of kings and Lord of lords. I got so caught up in worship of the supremacy of Christ that the entire congregation burst into exuberant praise of our Savior. Everyone in attendance at that special service remembers that particular sermon.

Even so, I was surprised when a member of the church told me that he had gone to Mexico on a business trip, and during the taxi ride to his hotel, he and the driver struck up a conversation about the Lord Jesus.

The taxi driver asked my church member, "Do you want to hear a great sermon that a friend sent me from America?"

Prophetic Signs

"Sure," he replied.

The driver proceeded play a tape of my sermon and the section in which Jesus is revealed in every book of the Bible.

My friend told the driver, "Hey, that's my pastor! I was there the morning he preached that sermon."

That sermon I had preached years before had traveled the world. So have millions of sermons in audio and written form. Technology has given us the means to preach the Gospel of Christ to the whole world. Global communication is a tool for us to tell the world about Jesus. Nations that are closed to missionaries—nations that outlaw churches and prevent the distribution of Bibles—cannot stop the good news of Jesus being preached through technology. Government persecution is conquered by Gospel preaching!

During the Great Tribulation, God will send an angel to proclaim the eternal Gospel. The apostle John in his visions of the future saw the sign of global missions being fulfilled:

> Then I saw another angel flying in midair, and he had the eternal gospel to proclaim to those who live on the earth—to every nation, tribe, language and people. He said in a loud voice, "Fear God and give him glory, because the hour of his judgment has come. Worship him who made the heavens, the earth, the sea and the springs of water."
>
> Revelation 14:6–7

The angel (meaning "messenger") flying in midair may describe satellites orbiting the earth broadcasting the Gospel with global communication to the whole world. Today the Word of God and the good news of Jesus is being proclaimed to all who live on the earth. So we are seeing this prophecy come to pass before our very eyes. When this sign happens, Jesus said, "Then the end will come" (Matthew 24:14).

The Fig Tree

My childhood home had a large fenced-in backyard that was great for playing outside. Our next-door neighbors had a fig tree right next to the fence. I would climb the fence and get into the tree. But the first time I got a fig to eat was a shock. I thought it would taste like a green plum—but it was awful. I still don't like figs—except for Fig Newtons!

Our neighbors' tree reminds me of Jesus' message about the last days:

> "Now learn this lesson from the fig tree: As soon as its twigs get tender and its leaves come out, you know that summer is near. Even so, when you see all these things, you know that it is near, right at the door. Truly I tell you, this generation will certainly not pass away until all these things have happened. Heaven and earth will pass away, but my words will never pass away."
>
> Matthew 24:32–35

The lesson of the fig tree is that the promise of Jesus' return is certain.

The fig tree does not represent the restoration of Israel in 1948, as some have suggested, although Israel's restoration was foretold by the prophets and serves as one of the greatest prophetic signs of our day. Rather, the fig tree parable refers to the fulfillment of all the signs Christ gave.

The fig tree coming into bloom, gradually but surely, is like the gradual unfolding of prophecy, as all will be fulfilled.

Prophetic Signs

Just as we can watch the leaves of the fig tree come out and discern that summer is near, we can watch prophetic signs and know that the end is near.

The word *generation* in Jesus' phrase "this generation will certainly not pass away" means race or people; and it refers, first of all, to the generation that witnessed the destruction of the Temple in AD 70. Jesus told His disciples, referring to His resurrection, "I tell you the truth, some who are standing here will not taste death before they see the kingdom of God come with power" (Mark 9:1 NIV 1984). That same generation, then, saw the Son of Man come with power when He was raised from the dead.

Ultimately there will be a generation to witness all the prophetic signs, as well as the glorious appearing of Jesus Christ. This is a dual prophecy, then, with a present as well as future application.

The main lesson of the fig tree analogy is to assure us that biblical prophecies are guaranteed. Jesus ends by declaring, "My words will never pass away." Every prophetic sign we see fulfilled assures us that God's promises concerning the end of the age and the dawn of eternity will surely come to pass.

TWO

FUTURE SHOCK

Future Shock is a 1970 bestselling book by futurist Alvin Toffler and his wife, Adelaide Farrell, in which they coined the term *future shock* to mean a personal and societal experience of too much change in too short a period of time.[1]

The ultimate future shock coming to this world, which will bring the greatest change in the shortest period of time, will be the return of Christ. Everything on earth will change immediately and drastically when He returns!

Associated with Jesus' return is a phenomenon we call the Rapture. We have all heard about the Rapture, and many books have been published and movies produced about it—but what is it?

The return of Jesus is a mystery. Paul the apostle explained: "Listen, I tell you a mystery: We will not all sleep, but we will all be changed—in a flash, in the twinkling of an eye, at the last trumpet" (1 Corinthians 15:51–52). That is future shock—when everything in the world changes in a flash and in the twinkling of an eye!

35

The twinkling of an eye takes less than half a second. We blink about 20 times a minute, or 1,200 blinks an hour, and 28,800 times a day. A half second is how fast our translation from this life into eternity will take. I don't think Paul was making a literal, scientific statement (although I thought you might enjoy this bit of science!), but he was saying that the Lord will come suddenly and decisively and take us to be with Him in heaven.

Early Christians believed that the return of the Lord could happen at any time. They woke up every day thinking that this could be the day our Lord returns. So should we. Like the early Church, we need to be "looking for the blessed hope and glorious appearing of our great God and Savior Jesus Christ" (Titus 2:13 NKJV). They did not get caught up with prophetic details and speculations, as we see in our day. We need to return to the simple scriptural view of Jesus' return, and avoid sensationalism. Let's celebrate the fact of His return and leave the details of His return to God.

Jesus could return at any moment and translate us to heaven. The apostle James said, "The Judge is standing at the door!" (James 5:9). Paul wrote, "The day of the Lord will come like a thief in the night" (1 Thessalonians 5:2). Jesus said, "Look, I come like a thief! Blessed is the one who stays awake and remains clothed, so as not to go naked and be shamefully exposed" (Revelation 16:15). And the Lord challenged us: "So you also must be ready, because the Son of Man will come at an hour when you do not expect him" (Matthew 24:44).

The Rapture

Jesus' return is the main event of the future. His return will take place in two phases. First He will take His people out of the world in the Rapture. Then, at the end of the age, He will return to the earth to set up His Kingdom and to rule and reign in righteousness. Some scholars deduce from Scripture that the Rapture will happen at the beginning of the Great Tribulation, and that Jesus will return at the battle of Armageddon to defeat the Antichrist. Other scholars view the Rapture and return of Christ as the same event occurring at the end of the Tribulation.

The term *Rapture* simply means to take away or to catch away suddenly:

> The Lord himself will come down from heaven, with a loud command, with the voice of the archangel and with the trumpet call of God, and the dead in Christ will rise first. After that, we who are still alive and are left will be caught up together with them in the clouds to meet the Lord in the air. And so we will be with the Lord forever. Therefore encourage one another with these words.
>
> 1 Thessalonians 4:16–18

While the word *Rapture* does not appear in the Bible, the concept certainly does. Paul said we will be "caught up" or snatched away suddenly.

Let's look more closely at this amazing passage about the Lord's return.

Personal Touch

The Lord himself. Jesus will not send a representative or angel to get us. He said, "I will come back and take you to be with me that you also may be where I am" (John 14:3). Jesus' return is a personal visit to this world to save His people from the final hour of judgment. The angels told the disciples, as they stood on the Mount of Olives gazing into the sky while Jesus ascended to heaven out of their sight: "This same Jesus, who has been taken from you into heaven, will come back in the same way you have seen him go into heaven" (Acts 1:11).

Some people think the return of Christ is only a metaphor about death, when the soul goes to heaven. Certainly when we die, we *will* go to heaven: "To be absent from the body [is] to be present with the Lord" (2 Corinthians 5:8 NKJV). And: "Blessed are the dead who die in the Lord from now on. . . . They will rest from their labor, for their deeds will follow them" (Revelation 14:13). But natural death is not the return of Jesus, as foretold in Scripture.

No, the Lord *Himself* will descend from heaven. Paul told us clearly, "We will not all sleep" (1 Corinthians 15:51). *Sleep* is the biblical term for death. That means that some people will not die a natural death. Instead they will be alive to see Jesus' return. I hope I am part of the generation that sees Him coming in the clouds of heaven! John the Revelator writes, "'Look, he is coming with the clouds,' and 'every eye will see him'" (Revelation 1:7). The return of Jesus is not a symbolic metaphor; it is a spiritual mystery bringing wonder and awe.

Heaven Opens

The Lord himself will come down from heaven. Jesus has to be in heaven in order to come down from heaven, and that is exactly where Jesus is now—reigning in heaven as Lord over creation and serving as our High Priest, who "always lives to intercede" for us (Hebrews 7:25). Jesus is our mediator, our bridge to God. He said, "No one comes to the Father except through me" (John 14:6).

Future Shock

The apostle John said: "We have an advocate with the Father—Jesus Christ, the Righteous One. He is the atoning sacrifice for our sins" (1 John 2:1–2). The word *advocate* means the defense attorney who speaks to God on our behalf. Since Jesus reigns in heaven, "we may approach God with freedom and confidence" (Ephesians 3:12).

Jesus is now seated "at the right hand of the throne of the Majesty in heaven" (Hebrews 8:1). But in God's perfect time, He will rise from His majestic throne of power and descend from heaven with a shout. He will come with power and great glory, surrounded by the angelic armies of heaven, to overthrow the forces of evil and establish His righteous rule on the earth, where "of the greatness of his government and peace there will be no end" (Isaiah 9:7).

When Satan tempted Jesus by offering Him the kingdoms of this world, Jesus turned the devil down. But when He comes again, He will take His rightful reign over the kingdoms of this world, when "at the name of Jesus every knee should bow, in heaven and on earth and under the earth, and every tongue acknowledge that Jesus Christ is Lord" (Philippians 2:10–11). Instead of Jesus bowing down to worship Satan, in order to gain the kingdoms of this world and their splendor, the world will bow down at His feet to worship Him as Savior and Lord of all.

> The seventh angel sounded his trumpet, and there were loud voices in heaven, which said: "The kingdom of the world has become the kingdom of our Lord and of his Messiah, and he will reign for ever and ever."
>
> Revelation 11:15

Angelic Announcement

The Lord himself will come down from heaven, with a loud command, with the voice of the archangel. The "loud command" is a shout of victory and praise. Shouting is an expression of worship that we see throughout the Bible. God says, "I will also clothe her priests with salvation, and her saints shall shout aloud for joy" (Psalm 132:16 NKJV). And: "Clap your hands, all you nations; shout to God with cries of joy" (Psalm 47:1). The shouting at Christ's return will be the joyful praise of God's people and the angels in heaven that the final day of God's plan for the world is coming to pass.

The archangel spoken of in this passage is Michael, the protector of God's people in times of distress. When Jesus was born, the angel of the Lord, God's personal messenger in the Old Testament, announced the Messiah's arrival to the shepherds in Bethlehem: "Suddenly a great company of the heavenly host appeared with the angel, praising God and saying, 'Glory to God in the highest heaven, and on earth peace to those on whom his favor rests'" (Luke 2:13–14).

Future Fanfare

The Lord himself will come down from heaven, with . . . the trumpet call of God. In music theory we call it fanfare—a short musical flourish, usually played by trumpets, to introduce a performance. God's fanfare is going to introduce King Jesus to the world.

My musical career began in the third grade when I joined the school band. I was first chair! I am still fond of the trumpet, even though I went on to study jazz and classical guitar. God Himself is a trumpet player! Here we read that Jesus' return will be announced by the trumpet call of God.

A pastor of a denomination once told me that they did not allow any musical instruments to be played in their worship services. I asked him why, since the Bible is filled with references to praising God with stringed instruments, flutes, trumpets, and more. He told me, "Since musical instruments aren't specifically mentioned in the New Testament, we don't use them in church."

I responded, "Air conditioning isn't mentioned in the New Testament, but I'm sure you have it in your church."

Yet the New Testament does mention musical instruments. The apostle Paul exhorts "speaking to one another with psalms, hymns, and songs from the Spirit" (Ephesians 5:19). The Greek word used here for *psalms* is *psalmos*, meaning a set piece of music such as a sacred ode, accompanied by the voice, harp, or other instruments.[2] The trumpet of the Lord will announce the return of Jesus. God loves music so much that He Himself is a trumpet player!

The sound of a trumpet appears in the Bible to announce a great divine moment. When Moses received the Law of God at Mount Sinai, it was accompanied by thunder, lightning, an earthquake, smoke and fire from the mountain, and a loud trumpet blast from heaven. The trumpet blast was divine in origin, and "grew louder and louder" (Exodus 19:19), until the sights and sounds of the presence of God overwhelmed the people of God at the base of the mountain (see Exodus 20:18).

Two silver trumpets were used in Israel's worship services for four purposes: to call an assembly, to set out from the camp into the wilderness, to summon the army to war, and to mark appointed festivals and feasts (see Numbers 10:2–10). Paul the apostle wrote that "the trumpet will sound, the

dead will be raised imperishable and we will be changed"
(1 Corinthians 15:52).

Rise Again

The Lord himself will come down from heaven . . . and the dead in Christ will rise first. I have been asked more questions about this phrase than anything else in the Bible concerning the Rapture and Christ's return. What does it mean that the dead in Christ will rise first? How could Paul say this, when the Scripture teaches that when a believer dies, his or her spirit goes to God in heaven at the moment of death?

Paul was not saying that the soul rests in the grave awaiting Christ's return. He was talking about the resurrection of the body. When we die, our soul is with God in heaven. When Jesus returns and restores the earth, we will receive an eternal, resurrected body like Jesus' resurrection body. Listen to this promise:

> Christ has indeed been raised from the dead, the firstfruits of those who have fallen asleep. . . . For as in Adam all die, so in Christ all will be made alive. But each in turn: Christ, the firstfruits; then, when he comes, those who belong to him. . . . For the perishable must clothe itself with the imperishable, and the mortal with immortality. When the perishable has been clothed with the imperishable, and the mortal with immortality, then the saying that is written will come true: "Death has been swallowed up in victory."
>
> 1 Corinthians 15:20, 22–23, 53–54

Our bodies are perishable. We are reminded of that fact when we look at ourselves in the mirror! But when Jesus returns and restores all things, our bodies will be perfect and eternal. We will receive glorified bodies just like the resurrection body of Jesus:

> Our citizenship is in heaven. And we eagerly await a Savior from there, the Lord Jesus Christ, who, by the power that enables him to bring everything under his control, will transform our lowly bodies so that they will be like his glorious body.
>
> Philippians 3:20–21

Today we place great emphasis on fashion, exercise, nutrition, and cosmetic improvements to keep ourselves fit. But God promises us new bodies in eternity when we live in a new heaven and a new earth. The new bodies we get in eternity will need no upkeep!

Caught Up

The Lord himself will come down from heaven. . . . After that, we who are still alive and are left will be caught up. While Christians have different views about the Rapture, one thing is certain: Many of us will be alive when Jesus returns. At that moment we will be "caught up." That phrase in the Latin version of the Bible is the word *rapture*.

The Rapture is the translation of God's people into heaven. The Rapture is illustrated in Scripture by people who experienced a personal rapture to heaven. Enoch was translated to heaven. "By faith Enoch was taken from this life, so that he did not experience death: 'He could not be found, because God had taken him away.' For before he was taken, he was commended as one who pleased God" (Hebrews 11:5; see Genesis 5:24). The prophet Elijah was taken to heaven in a chariot of fire (see 2 Kings 2:11). Jesus ascended to heaven after His resurrection enveloped in a cloud of glory (see Acts 1:9). And John the Revelator experienced a translation to heaven and saw God's throne:

> After this I looked, and there before me was a door standing open in heaven. And the voice I had first heard speaking to me like a trumpet said, "Come up here, and I will show you what must take place after this." At once I was in the Spirit, and there before me was a throne in heaven with [God the Father] sitting on it.
>
> Revelation 4:1–2

All these people were, in every sense of the word, caught up or raptured from earth into heaven. Their stories exemplify what it means for us to be "caught up together . . . to meet the Lord" in the clouds of the sky. The purpose of the Rapture is simply "to meet the Lord in the air."

What a meeting that will be! I have met important people in my life, but nothing can compare with meeting Jesus face to face.

Now we see Jesus by faith, as the apostle Peter wrote: "Though you have not seen him, you love him; and even though you do not see him now, you believe in him and are filled with an inexpressible and glorious joy" (1 Peter 1:8). But one day we will see Jesus in person: "We shall be like him, for we shall see him as he is" (1 John 3:2). And: "Now we see only a reflection as in a mirror; then we shall see face to face" (1 Corinthians 13:12). What an incredible day that will be!

Together Forever

We will be with the Lord forever. Every kid asks his or her parent, "How long is forever?" It is estimated that the Bible

Future Shock

contains some five thousand promises of God to His people. Here is the greatest of all His promises: "This is what he promised us—eternal life" (1 John 2:25). How can we have eternal life? The Bible tells us, "This is eternal life: that they know you, the only true God, and Jesus Christ, whom you have sent" (John 17:3).

The first college founded in America was Harvard College.

> According to a 1643 book titled "New Englands First Fruits," which contains the first mention of Harvard College, Puritan colonists founded Harvard "dreading to leave an illiterate ministry to the Churches, when our present Ministers shall lie in the Dust." Harvard's original motto was: "Truth for Christ and the Church."[3]

These words appear on many buildings on the campus.

John Harvard was a Cambridge-educated English minister who immigrated to New England and gave the first bequest to a Christian college (later to be called Harvard), including half of his estate and four hundred books from his own library, before his untimely death in 1638 at age thirty.[4]

The Harvard Graduate School Christian Fellowship still promotes the university's original "Rules and Precepts," adopted in 1646, one of which states: "Let every Student be plainly instructed, and earnestly pressed to consider well, the maine end of his life and studies, to know God and Jesus Christ which is eternal life."[5]

The primary reason Jesus came into the world was to save us from our sins and to give us eternal life. If you don't have eternal life, then you don't have a life. Any kind of life without eternal life is a half-lived life. You are not ready to live until you are ready to die, and you are not ready to die until you have eternal life in Christ.

Whatever happens to us in this life, and regardless of the trials we face, it all pales into insignificance in light of the fact that, in Paul's words, "we will be with the Lord forever." The promise of tomorrow gives us power for today.

There remains a challenge for us to consider: "Therefore encourage one another with these words." Let's not argue or debate about our Lord's return. Rather, we believers should encourage each other as we face personal problems and global unrest—because Christ is coming again! The future belongs to our God.

Get Ready

What difference does the promise of the Lord's return make in our lives? How should prophecy affect our lives now?

We need three things in order to live with purpose and power, and to be ready for the moment when an angelic voice shouts and the trumpet of God sounds.

Resilient Faith

Jesus asked, "When the Son of Man comes, will he find faith on the earth?" (Luke 18:8). Well, there is plenty of faith going around. Everybody talks about being "people of faith." But what faith? And what kind of faith is Jesus looking for? He is looking for a resilient faith that never gives up in discouragement, never runs out of resources, never gives in to defeat. He is looking for a vibrant and victorious faith. He is looking for faithfulness in His people.

Some people think the Rapture means an escape plan. But the Church has always faced times of tribulation. The

46

Rapture is not about escapism. Believers have suffered throughout the ages, and many are suffering for Christ today in their own tribulation. Real faith is not about escaping; it is about enduring trials, temptations, and tests. Faith means faithfulness to Jesus at all costs. When John the Revelator saw a vision of the coming Antichrist, he said, "This calls for patient endurance and faithfulness on the part of God's people" (Revelation 13:10). When we see the signs of the times being fulfilled, we need endurance and faithfulness.

When false Christs and false prophets appear, be faithful.

When you hear of wars and rumors of wars, be faithful.

When there are famines, earthquakes, and pestilences, be faithful.

When iniquity increases and the love of many grows cold, be faithful.

When you are persecuted for the sake of righteousness, be faithful.

When trials come your way, be faithful and you will pass the test.

When the apostles were tested in the refining fire of persecution, they rejoiced "because they had been counted worthy of suffering disgrace for the Name" (Acts 5:41).

Jesus is looking for resilient faith.

Radiant Hope

The return of Christ is called "the blessed hope" (Titus 2:13). The true Christian is an eternal optimist. We face uncertain times with hope, believing that "with God all things are possible" (Matthew 19:26). When we radiate hope, we give light to a darkened world. When we worship, work, and witness for Christ, we are truly being the light of the world.

Prophetic hope, not political hype, brings healing to the world. Our world lies in the darkness of fear and uncertainty. Now is our time to shine the light of hope in Christ. Just as Jesus' first coming into the world at Bethlehem was a divine light breaking into the world, so we bring Jesus into our world when we tell others about Him. "There will be no more gloom for those who were in distress. . . . The people walking in darkness have seen a great light; on those living in the land of deep darkness a light has dawned" (Isaiah 9:1–2).

In the words of the hymnwriter: "My hope is built on nothing less than Jesus' blood and righteousness. . . . On Christ the solid rock I stand!"

Responsive Love

One day the world as we know it will end. The Bible calls it "the end of the age" (Matthew 24:3). The word *age* means a time frame or period of history. The planet will not end by global warming, nuclear war, or environmental catastrophe. God will restore the earth, not remove it! "The age" refers to this present age of sin and suffering.

> *Then the end will come*, when [Jesus] hands over the kingdom to God the Father after he has destroyed all dominion, authority and power. For he must reign until he has put all his enemies under his feet.
>
> 1 Corinthians 15:24–25, emphasis added

This present age—not the world, but the present age—will end under the government of the Lord Jesus.

Notice carefully the words *then the end will come*. The end of this age is hopeful because it is the beginning of eternity with God on a new earth that is called "the home of righteousness" (2 Peter 3:13 NIV1984). What is true prophetically is true personally. After we have lived our lives on earth, if Jesus does not return in our lifetime, then the end will come for you and for me. As Amos the prophet said, "Prepare to meet your God" (Amos 4:12).

When the end comes for you, will you go to heaven? You can know you have eternal life by trusting Christ as your Savior and confessing Him as your Lord. "Believe in the Lord Jesus, and you will be saved" (Acts 16:31).

The promise of Christ's return, and the fact that the end will come—prophetically for the world and personally for every individual—compels us to share the Gospel of Christ so others, too, can have eternal life in Him. When we take the Lord's return to heart, we, like Jesus, will be "moved with compassion" when He saw the crowds (Matthew 9:36 NKJV). Why? Because "Christ's love compels us" (2 Corinthians 5:14). His love compels us to "go into all the world and preach the gospel to all creation" (Mark 16:15).

A friend of mine told me about an opportunity he had to share his faith while on a cruise. Dan met a man on board ship, and they started talking. Just when the man was about to leave, Dan felt compelled to tell him about his faith in Jesus. Then he asked him, "Do you mind if I ask you a spiritual question?"

"No," he replied. "Go right ahead."

Dan asked, "If you were to die today, do you know you would go to heaven?"

The man replied straightforwardly, "No, I don't know that I would go to heaven."

Dan was surprised and glad for the man's honesty. He continued, "Would you like for me to share with you how I came to know that I have eternal life?"

"Yes, I would."

So Dan took the opportunity to tell the man about Jesus Christ and God's plan of salvation through Him.

As we eagerly await our Savior from heaven, may we be compelled by the love of Christ to tell others that they, too, can have eternal life in Christ.

THREE

ISRAEL UNDER SIEGE

On May 15, 1948, the United Nations passed a resolution declaring Israel an independent state with full rights of self-government. United States President Harry Truman was the first world leader to officially recognize Israel as a legitimate Jewish state only eleven minutes after its creation. The attention of the world continues to be focused on Israel because of the war caused by the Hamas terrorist attack of October 2023 and the escalation of the conflict.

In the last days, Jesus said, Israel will take center stage in world history, with a great war focused on Jerusalem. Today Jerusalem is under siege by Hamas and Hezbollah and their patron, Iran. These terrorist regimes are motivated by Islamic jihad with a desire to exterminate the Jewish people and seize their rightful homeland. The chant "From the river to the sea" by radical groups, even in America, are chants to destroy the state of Israel, from the Jordan River to the Mediterranean Sea. The same radical groups also chant, "Death to America."

Israel plays a strategic role in biblical prophecy regarding the Second Coming of Christ. The restoration of Israel is one of the greatest signs of Christ's return. On the Mount of Olives, Jesus prophesied about the last days to His disciples before He went to the cross. Jesus wants us to know the future and final chapter of human history so we rest assured that God is in control.

In the first chapter we looked at the questions the disciples asked after Jesus prophesied the destruction of the Temple in Jerusalem: When will this happen? What will be the sign of Your coming and of the end of the age? And we discussed the prophetic signs Jesus gave them: false messiahs and false prophets; wars and revolutions; international political conflict with nation against nation; ecological disturbances with earthquakes, famines, and pestilences in various places; fearful events and great signs from heaven; and the persecution of God's people.

Jesus also gave the Israel sign: "Jerusalem will be trampled on by the Gentiles until the times of the Gentiles are fulfilled" (Luke 21:24). The term *Gentiles* simply means "nations." Jesus continued, "At that time they will see the Son of Man coming in a cloud with power and great glory" (verse 27).

The Israel sign, Jesus tells us, is an indicator of His return.

The Creation of Israel

The history of the Jewish people is one marked by the fingerprints of God. They have endured rejection, invasion, captivity, and dispersion, yet they occupy center-stage in modern history. God's covenant to Abraham still stands:

> "I will make you into a great nation, and I will bless you;
> I will make your name great, and you will be a blessing. I
> will bless those who bless you, and whoever curses you I will
> curse; and *all peoples* on earth will be blessed through you."
>
> Genesis 12:2–3, emphasis added

God promised Abraham and his descendants the land where they live today. The people of Israel do not occupy Palestine. The nation of Israel began with God's call and covenant with Abraham. The Holy Land is their birthright, and declared by international law, backed by the 1948 UN resolution, to be their natural homeland. The Jews were dispersed by the Assyrians and Babylonians but today have returned home, as God promised.

Further, the Temple in Jerusalem was for all nations. God declared,

> Foreigners who bind themselves to the LORD to minister to
> him, to love the name of the LORD, and to be his servants
> . . . these I will bring to my holy mountain and give them
> joy in my house of prayer . . . for my house will be called a
> house of prayer for all nations.
>
> Isaiah 56:6–7, emphasis added

The reference to "all nations" refers to Jesus bringing salvation to the whole world. His Gospel is for people everywhere. Jesus commanded His disciples, "Go and make disciples of all nations" (Matthew 28:19). And He declared, "This gospel of the kingdom will be preached in the whole world as a testimony to all nations, and then the end will come" (Matthew 24:14). Abraham is the father of the faithful—all who trust in the one true God and in Jesus Christ, our Savior.

I heard a story once about the Russian czar Peter the Great, under whose reign a pastor was imprisoned for his faith. The czar summoned him one day and asked, "Can you give me one infallible proof to verify the Bible?"

"Yes," he replied. "The Jew."

The return of the Jews to their homeland in 1948 and their global power today are a testimony to fulfilled prophecy.

Jewish history is the story of the faithfulness of God. Their history can be traced along the following dateline:

2000 BC Abraham is called from Ur of the Chaldees to the Promised Land.

1450 BC Moses leads the people out of Egypt in the exodus.

1400 BC Joshua leads the conquest of Canaan.

1380 BC The judges rule for 330 years.

1053 BC Saul is inaugurated as the first king of Israel.

1013 BC The Davidic kingdom is established and the covenant given.

930 BC Israel is divided after Solomon's death.

722 BC Israel (Northern Kingdom) is invaded by Assyria and exiled.

586 BC Judah (Southern Kingdom) is invaded by Babylon and exiled.

539 BC Jews begin to return to Jerusalem after Babylonian captivity.

165 BC Jews rededicate the Temple at the first Hanukkah after defeating the Seleucid Empire (modern-day Syria).

63 BC Rome rises to power and takes control of Israel.

AD 70	Rome destroys Jerusalem and the Temple under Titus.
AD 135	The Roman emperor Hadrian invades Israel and renames it Palestine.
AD 1882	The first group of Jewish colonists settle in Palestine.
AD 1914	England, France, and Russia declare war on the Ottoman Turks.
AD 1917	Military forces under General Allenby advance into Palestine.
AD 1918	The Balfour Declaration is published, with the British committing to support the Jewish state.
AD 1948	The United Nations recognizes Israel as an independent state.
AD 1948	The war of independence is fought against seven Arab states.
AD 1956	The Sinai campaign is fought against Egypt, Jordan, and Syria.
AD 1967	The Six-Day War results in the Jewish restoration of Jerusalem.
AD 1973	The Yom Kippur (Day of Atonement) War is fought against a coalition of Arab states.
AD 2000	Israel becomes the site of violence by the terrorism of the Palestine Liberation Organization.
AD 2023	Israel is attacked by Hamas, spiraling into war on two fronts.

Israeli statesman David Ben-Gurion, speaking on the evening of Israel's independence, put this historic event into prophetic perspective:

In the land of Israel, the Jewish people came into being. In this land was shaped their religious and national character.

Here they lived in sovereign independence. Here they created a culture of national and universal import, and here they wrote and gave the Bible to the world. Though exiled, the Jewish people remained faithful to the land, never ceasing to pray for their return. . . . This has now come about.

They reclaimed the wilderness, revived their language. . . . They sought peace, yet were prepared to defend themselves. They brought the blessings of progress to all inhabitants of the country. . . . By virtue of the natural and historic right of the Jewish people and of the resolution of the General Assembly of the United Nations, we hereby proclaim the establishment of the Jewish state in Palestine, to be called the State of Israel.[1]

The Conflict of Jerusalem

While the Hebrew name for Jerusalem, *Yerushalayim*, means "possession of peace," the city has been marked by endless conflict. The times of the Gentiles—the period when Jesus prophesied that Jerusalem will be "trampled on . . . until the times of the Gentiles is fulfilled"—is now, the Church Age, from Pentecost to the return of Christ.

What is the history of Jerusalem that makes it the focal point of history?

The Development of Jerusalem

Melchizedek was the king of Salem ("king of peace") and priest of God, to whom Abraham gave a tithe. Jerusalem is located on Mount Moriah, where Abraham took Isaac. David established this city as his capital, also called the city of God and the city of the great king. This is where Solomon built the Temple of God and the Holy of Holies.

56

Calvary, outside the gates of Jerusalem, is where Jesus died. The Mount of Olives, east of Jerusalem, is where Jesus ascended into heaven. Jerusalem was the birthplace of the Church at Pentecost with the outpouring of the Holy Spirit. Jerusalem is the launchpad of world evangelization (see Acts 1:8). Jerusalem is the city where Jesus will return (see Zechariah 14:1–4). And Jerusalem represents the heavenly city, the New Jerusalem (see Hebrews 12:22; Revelation 21:1–5).

The Destruction of Jerusalem

Jesus' prophecy that the Temple would be totally destroyed—"not one stone . . . left on another" (Luke 21:6)—came to pass during the Roman wars of AD 66–70. Later, in AD 135, Emperor Hadrian attacked Israel, dispersing the people to other nations and renaming the land Palestine, a name taken from the word *Philistine*, the ancient enemy of God's people. Hadrian wanted to cancel Jewish history, leaving no mention of the name Israel. He called the land Palestine out of spite for the Jewish people and their national heritage. The Jews were scattered around the world.

The tragedy of the Jewish–Roman Wars and the loss of the Temple would eventually prepare the nation for a new day:

> For the Jews a new dispensation had begun with the passing of that which had been their central part of worship. They were to be scattered now among the nations, but they would take with them their writings and their religion. They would survive because they had a unique role in human history. And the Jerusalem that now lay about them in ruins would rise again because it too was an integral part of that uniqueness.[2]

The Destiny of Israel

The twentieth century witnessed the return of the Jewish people to their homeland. Israel's rebirth as a world power was foretold and is now fulfilled.

Isaiah prophesied that the Jewish people would "rebuild the ancient ruins. . . . All who see them will acknowledge that they are a people the LORD has blessed" (Isaiah 61:4, 9). Ezekiel prophesied that the Jewish people would be cleansed and resettle their towns, rebuild the ruins, and be like the Garden of Eden (see Ezekiel 36:33–36). The prophet Amos foretold the return of the Jewish people to their homeland. In God's words: "I will bring my people Israel back from exile. They will rebuild the ruined cities . . . plant vineyards. . . . I will plant Israel in their own land, never again to be uprooted from the land I have given them" (Amos 9:14–15). Zechariah prophesied that Jerusalem would become "an immovable rock for all the nations. All who try to move it will injure themselves" (Zechariah 12:3).

Jesus said that Jerusalem will be at the center of world history before His return: "When you see Jerusalem being surrounded by armies, you will know that its desolation is near" (Luke 21:20). While this prophecy spoke historically to the Roman invasion of AD 70, it also points forward to the Second Coming, when Christ will return to Jerusalem: "On that day his feet will stand on the Mount of Olives, east of Jerusalem. . . . Then the LORD my God will come, and all the holy ones [saints and angels] with him" (Zechariah 14:4–6). Jude declared, "See, the Lord is coming with thousands upon thousands of his holy ones to judge everyone" (Jude 14–15).

The apostle John, describing the Lord's return, said that the Antichrist and his armies "will wage war against the Lamb, but the Lamb will triumph over them because he is Lord of lords and King of kings—and with him will be his called, chosen and faithful followers" (Revelation 17:14).

Zechariah continued his prophecy: "The LORD will be king over the whole earth. . . . But Jerusalem will be raised up high . . . and will remain in its place. It will be inhabited; never again will it be destroyed" (Zechariah 14:9–11).

All these prophecies explain why Jerusalem stands at the center of world history today.

Jesus ascended to heaven from the Mount of Olives located outside the wall of Jerusalem. And He will return to that very place, as the angels told the disciples: "This same Jesus, who has been taken from you into heaven, will come back in the same way you have seen him go into heaven" (Acts 1:11).

In 1917 there were fewer than 25,000 Jews in the Holy Land. By 1945, at the end of World War II, there were 500,000. Today, 7.2 million Jews comprise 73.2 percent of the population, along with Arabs, who have often lived together in peace.[3]

The Deliverance of Israel

The Church Age in which we live is considered to be "the times of the Gentiles," as in Jesus' statement, "Jerusalem will be trampled on by the Gentiles until the times of the Gentiles are fulfilled" (Luke 21:24). All nations have the opportunity to hear the Gospel and come into the covenant of salvation (see Matthew 24:14). During the last days Israel will rise to power and the Gentiles will no longer rule over her. Today we see Israel rising to prominence and Jerusalem capturing the attention of the world. By the sovereignty of God, Israel prevails over her persecutors and political enemies.

Are "the times of the Gentiles" drawing to a close? Does the rise of Jerusalem point to the Second Coming of Jesus?

The times of the Gentiles will reach their height during the Great Tribulation, when the Antichrist invades Jerusalem. He will desecrate the city and the Temple by committing what Scripture calls "the abomination that causes desolation" (Matthew 24:15). Jesus' reference to the Temple leads many to conclude that an actual Temple will be constructed in Jerusalem on the Temple Mount, which still exists. Then the Antichrist will meet his end when Jesus returns from heaven with His army of saints and angels and establishes His throne on earth at Jerusalem.

The Revelator heard voices in heaven saying loudly, "The kingdoms of this world have become the kingdoms of our Lord and of His Christ, and He shall reign forever and ever!" (Revelation 11:15 NKJV).

The Return of Christ

The fact (not fantasy!) of Jesus' return is central in the Bible. The New Testament contains 318 prophecies of Jesus' return. He will return when all the prophetic signs are fulfilled:

> "At that time, they will see the Son of Man coming in a cloud with power and great glory. When these things begin to take place, stand up and lift up your heads, for your redemption is drawing near."
>
> Luke 21:27–28

Israel Under Siege

Jesus came the first time to redeem the world from sin. He will come the second time to rule the world in righteousness. When He came the first time, He was meek and lowly of heart, but He will return as Judge of all the earth. When He came the first time, He was born in a manger and wrapped in cloths of linen, but when He returns, He will be clothed with glory. When He came the first time, He was given a reed for a scepter, but when He returns, He will rule the nations with a rod of iron. When He came the first time, He wore a crown of thorns, but He will return crowned with many crowns. When He came the first time, He was rejected, mocked, and crucified, but when He returns, every knee will bow before Him and every tongue confess, "Jesus is Lord!"

When I first visited the National Gallery of Art in Washington, D.C., I was awed by the majestic paintings. The closer I got to a painting, the more the detailed strokes of the painter's brush looked ambiguous. But when I stood back and saw the big picture, I was captivated by the scene.

The details of Bible prophecy give us a magnificent portrait of hope.

Take the Challenge

How should current world events that parallel biblical prophecy affect us? Jesus gave us this word of assurance in anxious times: "When these things begin to happen, look up and lift up your heads, because your redemption draws near" (Luke 21:28 NKJV).

Christians need to stand up for Christ. Make a stand for Jesus with your family, friends, and community. When you are challenged about your faith, stand, and having done all, stand, as Paul wrote: "Put on the full armor of God, so that when the day of evil comes, you may be able to stand your ground, and after you have done everything, to stand" (Ephesians 6:13). Make a stand and keep standing. Your stance is the story of Jesus' salvation in your life.

When Jesus said, "Lift up your heads," He meant to keep your courage. David described God as "my glory, the One who lifts my head high" (Psalm 3:3). And David calls us to worship the Lord by saying: "Lift up your heads, you gates; be lifted up, you ancient doors, that the King of glory may come in. Who is this King of glory? The LORD strong and mighty, the LORD mighty in battle" (Psalm 24:7–8). Hold your head high and don't allow your heart to be troubled by world events. God is in control!

Jesus also tells us to remember the final outcome of history: "Your redemption draws near." This is both a prophetic and a personal promise. Whatever you are facing today, your redemption, your salvation, your healing, your restoration— all are drawing near!

Jesus is coming again, but His greatest coming is when He comes to you and knocks on the door of your heart and you welcome Him in. Listen to Jesus' invitation to you: "Here I am! I stand at the door and knock. If anyone hears my voice and opens the door, I will come in and eat with that person, and they with me" (Revelation 3:20).

FOUR

THE DAYS OF NOAH RETURN

Current world conditions make us ask, Are we living in the last days before the return of Christ? In addition to the Israel sign, one of the most intriguing indications of Jesus' return is the return of the days of Noah. Jesus said, "As it was in the days of Noah, so it will be at the coming of the Son of Man" (Matthew 24:37). History will repeat itself. As it was, so it will be.

Everyone has heard the story of Noah and the Ark. The great Flood in Noah's day occurred at an early point in human history, when the population of the world was scarce, and "every inclination of the thoughts of the human heart was only evil all the time" (Genesis 6:5). No one knows when the Flood came or how many people were living at that time. The Garden of Eden had been located between the Tigris and Euphrates Rivers. The general area of Mesopotamia was the cradle of civilization. The earth was changing. There was no rain at the time, but a mist covered the earth.

"The earth was corrupt in God's sight and was full of violence" (Genesis 6:11), so God warned Noah of a great Flood and told him to build the Ark. A time frame of 120 years passed from the warning God gave Noah until the actual Flood. (People lived longer lifespans before the Flood, while afterward God limited mankind's lifespan, due to sin.) Noah was "a preacher of righteousness" to his generation (2 Peter 2:5).

The name *Noah* means "comfort"; and as "a preacher of righteousness," he lived up to his name. But the people carried on with life as usual. They saw the mighty Ark being constructed over many years, but were surely unimpressed, being unfamiliar with rain, and probably derisive, even while seeing his faith in action. Faith without works is dead (James 2:26). It is easy to ignore somebody's words, but when that person is building a huge boat, you should take him seriously and consider the prediction of a flood.

But God's judgment was impending. Sadly they ignored the evidence of the message—the building of the Ark.

Flood Details

Maybe we should stop right here and consider if the Flood was literal and not metaphorical. First of all, the fact that Jesus refers to Noah's day and the Flood—which, He said, "came and took them all away" (Matthew 24:39)—assures us that the Flood actually occurred. The One who claimed, "I am the truth," would not mislead us.

There is also scientific evidence of the Flood from geology; and many cultures and religions record a flood story.

Did the Flood cover the entire earth? Scientifically that proposition poses a problem. It does not have to have covered every square inch of the earth's surface, but only where people lived, in a limited geographical area.

Underwater surveyors, led by Robert Ballard, the renowned oceanographer who located the *Titanic* and other sunken ships of the twentieth century, have discovered an ancient coastline at a depth of 450 feet below sea level. Dr. Ballard, who has participated in 120 deep sea expeditions, commented about a structure that could possibly be the Ark: "Artifacts at the site are clearly well preserved, with carved wooden beams, wooden branches and stone tools collapsed amongst the mud matrix of the structure." He continued: "We know that there was a sudden and dramatic change from a freshwater lake to a saltwater sea 7,000 years ago. And we know that as a result of that flood a vast amount of land went underwater."[1]

The Ballard team was working from a theory about the biblical flood of antiquity propounded by two marine geologists from Columbia University in New York, William Ryan and Walter Pitman, in their book *Noah's Flood: The New Scientific Discoveries about the Event That Changed History*. Dr. Ballard does not think the actual shipwreck will be found. "It's foolish to think you will ever find a ship," he said. "But can you find people who were living? Can you find their villages that are underwater now? And the answer is yes."[2]

Instant Replay

The story of the Flood teaches us about sin, its consequences, and, most importantly, the saving grace of God, which Noah and his family experienced.

The people in Noah's day could have experienced saving grace if they had repented and honored God. "The Lord is not slow in keeping his promise, as some understand slowness. Instead he is patient with you, not wanting anyone to perish, but everyone to come to repentance" (2 Peter 3:9). The Gospel is clear: God does not want anyone to perish but for everyone to come to repentance and salvation.

The people of Noah's day lived in perilous times but did not realize it. They went about life as usual:

> "In the days before the flood, people were eating and drinking, marrying and giving in marriage, up to the day Noah entered the ark; and they knew nothing about what would happen until the flood came and took them all away."
>
> Matthew 24:37–39

The people ignored Noah, "a preacher of righteousness," as well as the physical evidence in plain view—the building of a great Ark. Today people tune out the voice of Christian pastors and drive by churches every Sunday to carry on with business as usual. Crowds gather in churches at Easter and Christmas, but people treat the Sundays in between these great holy days as any other day of the week. They may even attend a Christian event (which is noteworthy), but they do not have an experience with God. When we go to the house of God, we need to let Christ enter our hearts.

So Noah's generation was swept away by the Flood. The great deluge "did not spare the ancient world when [God] brought the flood on its ungodly people, but God protected Noah, a preacher of righteousness, and seven others" (2 Peter 2:5). Noah preached righteousness—the right way to live in relationship to God and others—and he still inspires us to live a righteous life in an unrighteous world as a witness to save others. We witness for Christ both in the way we speak and in the way we live. Our lives as well as our words are a living witness.

The people scoffed at Noah's message of salvation. They went beyond ignoring the Gospel to the point of ridiculing the threat of God's judgment. The apostle Peter, reflecting on Noah's day, wrote that people will likewise ignore and scoff at the promise of Jesus' return:

> Above all, you must understand that in the last days scoffers will come, scoffing and following their own evil desires. They will say, "Where is this 'coming' he promised? Ever since our ancestors died, everything goes on as it has since the beginning of creation." But they deliberately forget that long ago by God's word the heavens came into being and the earth was formed out of water and by water. By these waters also the world of that time was deluged and destroyed. By the same word the present heavens and earth are reserved for fire, being kept for the day of judgment and destruction of the ungodly.
>
> 2 Peter 3:3–7

The Days of Noah

What were the days of Noah like? More importantly, what were the people of his day like? Let's go back to the story of Noah in the book of Genesis and see how his times parallel our times.

> The LORD saw how great the wickedness of the human race had become on the earth, and that every inclination of the thoughts of the human heart was only evil all the time. . . .

Now the earth was corrupt in God's sight and was full of violence. God saw how corrupt the earth had become, for all the people on earth had corrupted their ways.

Genesis 6:5, 11–12

What was it like in Noah's day?

Days of Wickedness

Wow! The first descriptive phrase of the people's character is "great wickedness." Does history really repeat itself? According to Jesus, it does. He said, "As it was . . . so it will be" (Matthew 24:37). Those days have indeed returned.

Jesus' words of history repeating itself resemble the remarks of Winston Churchill in his famous Iron Curtain speech, "The Sinews of Peace":

> The dark ages may return, the Stone Age may return on the gleaming wings of science, and what might now shower immeasurable material blessings upon mankind, may even bring about its total destruction. Beware, I say; time may be short. Do not let us take the course of allowing events to drift along until it is too late.[3]

Days of Evil

"The LORD saw . . . that every inclination of the thoughts of the human heart was only evil all the time" (Genesis 6:5). When people tell me as a pastor that the world is worse than it has ever been, as though the times we are living in are hopeless, I remind them of Noah's day and say, "It's not that bad."

What a sad description of humanity made in God's glorious image! Every imagination of the human heart was on evil continually. No wonder God's heart was filled with pain. He created us with vast potential, and we squandered it away.

Days of Violence

"The earth was corrupt in God's sight and was full of violence" (Genesis 6:11). We live in a world of wars and rumors of wars. As I write, Ukraine is experiencing war after the invasion of Russia, and Israel is engulfed in war with the assault of the terrorist organizations Hamas and Hezbollah, backed by Iran.

America is witnessing unprecedented violence in our major cities, as some leading politicians have defunded the police, reformed bail to eliminate bail for violent offenders, refused to enforce the law, declined to prosecute crime, permitted stealing and looting as minor offenses, and released violent criminals. Millions of illegal aliens have been allowed and even encouraged to enter the U.S., some with criminal backgrounds, some from violent gangs, some even listed on terrorist watchlists. Some European countries that made the same mistakes have suffered the consequences and are changing their policies, in order to reestablish law and order and achieve peaceful and prosperous lives for their citizens.

Days of Visionless People

The word *vision* in the Old Testament means a revelation based on the Word of God. For example, Proverbs 29:18 says, "Where there is no revelation [or vision], the people cast off restraint." In the context of the Flood, Peter called Noah "a preacher of righteousness" (2 Peter 2:5), but no one listened. Jesus said that the people of Noah's day "knew nothing about what would happen until the flood came and took them all away" (Matthew 24:39).

69

How could they not know? Noah told them the Flood was coming, and he built the Ark as a testimony to the truth. But the people refused to listen. The word *ignorance* is related to the word *ignore*. They ignored God's invitation to repentance.

When Hurricane Katrina was threatening to devastate New Orleans in 2005, the governor warned that the great storm would bring a surge of floodwater from the Gulf of Mexico. Yet many people did not take the warning to heart and decided to stay where they were. Tragically nearly fourteen hundred people perished when they could have been saved.

Stephen, the first martyr, told the religious leaders trying him for heresy, "You always resist the Holy Spirit!" (Acts 7:51).

Such were the days of Noah.

The Heart of God

Now we get a glimpse into God's heart before He decided to send the Flood: "The LORD regretted that he had made human beings on the earth, and his heart was deeply troubled" (Genesis 6:6). The heart is the center of intellect, will, and emotions. God made us in His image. His heart, like ours, feels both positive and negative emotions. We have spiritual as well as physical hearts. That is why King David is called a man after God's own heart—because he had an emotional connection with God, not just an intellectual faith.

The story of Noah is a story of grace as well as judgment. The only reason judgment came is that the people forfeited God's grace. Noah, on the other hand, found grace in the eyes of the Lord and was a preacher of the grace of God for the salvation of the world.

God finds no pleasure in judgment. "Who is a God like you, who pardons sin and forgives the transgression of the remnant of his inheritance? You do not stay angry forever but delight to show mercy" (Micah 7:18). "Return to the LORD your God, for he is gracious and compassionate, slow to anger and abounding in love, and he relents from sending calamity" (Joel 2:13). Judgment includes both the acts of God and the natural consequences of human sin. We reap what we sow.

But God's heart is filled with pain for humanity—the pain of love and compassion. Jesus, seeing the crowds, "had compassion on them, because they were harassed and helpless, like sheep without a shepherd" (Matthew 9:36). Later, seeing another crowd, "he had compassion on them and healed their sick" (Matthew 14:14).

I am sure you have said, "My heart hurts for that person." We, like Jesus, are moved by the sight of human suffering and sinfulness and want to share the hope we have in Him. We are the Noah Generation today. Jesus sends us, just as God sent Noah, empowered by the Holy Spirit, to warn our world of the coming flood and to witness of the wonders of grace.

Noah was both a warning and a witness to his world. The Ark was a physical structure serving to warn and to witness to the way of salvation. The grace of God is more powerful than any sin, guilt, or failure. "Where sin increased, grace increased all the more" (Romans 5:20). Our God is "not willing that any should perish but that all should come to repentance" (2 Peter 3:9 NKJV).

But Noah's generation accepted sin as a normal state of living. Nothing was considered irreverent or immoral. Human cultures and societies have crumbled throughout history when mankind disregards God and His moral law for a just and peaceful society. The fall of the Roman Empire is well documented as a culture that perished from its immoral and indulgent practices. The days of Noah also describe a culture that inverts right and wrong: "Woe to those who call evil good, and good evil; who put darkness for light, and light for darkness; who put bitter for sweet, and sweet for bitter!" (Isaiah 5:20 NKJV).

Sin, missing the mark of God's will for our lives, is the root problem of our personal and societal problems: "All have sinned and fall short of the glory of God" (Romans 3:23). Sin is transgressing God's law. All of us are born with a sinful nature, and we also commit sin. We can cure many illnesses and psychological disorders, but we cannot cure the spiritual disease of sin. Before his conversion, Paul the apostle thought he could cure sin by keeping religious laws. He was sadly mistaken and wrote, "No one will be declared righteous in God's sight by the works of the law; rather, through the law we become conscious of our sin" (Romans 3:20).

The good news is that Jesus came to save us and to cure us from our sins. Jesus is the Great Physician! Paul went on to tell us that just as all have sinned, "all are justified freely by his grace through the redemption that came by Christ Jesus" (Romans 3:24). The word *justified* means to be declared righteous in God's sight. No wonder Paul wrote of his own experience with Jesus: "Here is a trustworthy saying that deserves full acceptance: Christ Jesus came into the world to save sinners—of whom I am the worst" (1 Timothy 1:15).

Faith Formula

Noah and his family were not saved from the Flood because he was better than everybody else. Noah did not preach self-righteousness, but exemplified the truth that righteousness comes from a right relationship with God through faith and repentance. Noah demonstrated what Abraham lived out many years later, when he lived in a culture of idolatry:

> If, in fact, Abraham was justified by works, he had something to boast about—but not before God. What does Scripture say? "Abraham believed God, and it was credited to him as righteousness."
>
> Romans 4:2–3

In the same way, when you and I trust in Jesus as Savior, we are justified and made righteous in God's eyes. "Since we have been justified through faith, we have peace with God through our Lord Jesus Christ" (Romans 5:1).

One of our greatest misunderstandings is that salvation in the Old Testament came by works and by following the Law, but that in the New Testament, it came by grace. That is simply not true. The Law of God as codified in the Ten Commandments did not exist in Noah's day. The only Law was the law of conscience, in which God writes His law on our hearts so we know right from wrong:

> When Gentiles, who do not have the law, do by nature things required by the law, they are a law for themselves, even though they do not have the law. They show that the requirements of the law are written on their hearts, their consciences also bearing witness, and their thoughts sometimes accusing them

and at other times even defending them. This will take place on the day when God judges people's secrets through Jesus Christ.

Romans 2:14–16

God holds us accountable for His revelation of Himself and His truth in our consciences. The people of Noah's day ignored their consciences and silenced the inner voice that distinguishes right from wrong. Paul the apostle wrote that in the last days, too, people will ignore their consciences:

The Spirit clearly says that in later times some will abandon the faith and follow deceiving spirits and things taught by demons. Such teachings come through hypocritical liars, whose consciences have been seared as with a hot iron.

1 Timothy 4:1–2

As a boy, I liked to help my mom with her work. I would stand by the ironing board and watch her iron shirts and see the steam come from the iron and hear the sound of the hot iron on the clothes as she pressed them to perfection. I think of her hot iron when I read this Scripture describing people whose consciences are seared. The human heart can become hard like a stiffly starched dress shirt, no longer feeling convicted of right and wrong or truth from error. Truly the days of Noah have returned.

God is a God of grace and does everything for humanity out of His grace.

"Noah found grace in the eyes of the LORD" (Genesis 6:8 NKJV). God longed to extend His grace to everyone in that day, just as He had to Noah. Grace warned the people to repent and to save themselves. But they refused His grace, to their own peril. Only Noah, who "walked faithfully with God" (Genesis 6:9), responded to God's grace with faith. When we receive the grace of God in Christ, He gives us the power to live right and blameless among the people of our times. As Christians we desire to be conformed to Christ, not to culture. Mostly importantly, we can walk with God.

I love the image of walking with God. Jesus came to restore our relationship with God, which was broken by sin, so we can walk with God. What an amazing truth! We can walk with Him in this life and know that He is walking with us to provide for us, to protect us, and to prosper us.

When we walk with God, we become living witnesses to others of the greatest life possible. When we live the way God intended, Jesus will improve every aspect of life. "Righteousness exalts a nation, but sin condemns any people" (Proverbs 14:34). The same is true for individuals. Righteousness exalts everything in life to its highest potential, while sin brings everything down to the lowest common denominator. Paul wrote, "I will show you the most excellent way" (1 Corinthians 12:31). The most excellent way of love is the way of Jesus. When you follow Jesus, you will live the most excellent way.

So Noah walked with God. His walk became his witness. Noah witnessed by his words and actions both. If people refused to listen to his words, they could see the witness of his works as he built the Ark. The world was judged when it could have been justified by faith in God. People experience judgment when they reject justification.

We need to follow the example of Noah, a man who believed and built the Ark of safety, as both believers and builders. Paul wrote these words of encouragement:

You yourselves are our letter, written on our hearts, known and read by everyone. You show that you are a letter from Christ, the result of our ministry, written not with ink but with the Spirit of the living God, not on tablets of stone but on tablets of human hearts.

2 Corinthians 3:2–3

You and I are living letters, emails, and text messages for Christ. If people stop listening as you share Christ with them, remember your life, for Christ continues to witness to them, so that "if any of them do not believe the word, they may be won over without words . . . when they see the purity and reverence of your lives" (1 Peter 3:1–2).

What Did Noah Save?

The story of Noah is the story of the entire Bible—God's plan of salvation from sin and judgment. The faith of Noah meant the salvation of the world:

By faith Noah, when warned about things not yet seen, in holy fear built an ark to save his family. By his faith he condemned the world and became heir of the righteousness that is in keeping with faith.

Hebrews 11:7

What did Noah save?

His Family

The purpose of the Ark was to save Noah's family. Your faith in Christ provides a spiritual covering for your own family. As Paul and Silas said to the Philippian jailer, "Believe in the Lord Jesus, and you will be saved—you and your household" (Acts 16:31). And listen to this promise: "The unbelieving husband has been sanctified through his wife, and the unbelieving wife has been sanctified through her believing husband. Otherwise your children would be unclean, but as it is, they are holy" (1 Corinthians 7:14).

As you provide a spiritual covering for your family, God will use you to get them into the Ark of safety, who is Jesus.

The Animal Kingdom

Noah also saved the animal kingdom. It is interesting that the animals were willing to enter the Ark, but not the people of the world. No wonder Job counseled his friend:

> "Ask the animals, and they will teach you, or the birds in the sky, and they will tell you; or speak to the earth, and it will teach you, or let the fish in the sea inform you. Which of all these does not know that the hand of the LORD has done this? In his hand is the life of every creature and the breath of all mankind."
>
> Job 12:7–10

The intuition and instinct of the animals were more in tune with God than the intellect and hearts of people who tuned God out.

His Faith

Noah saved his own faith. Hebrews 11:7 says, "By faith Noah . . ." He lived by faith in a faithless generation.

Our faith is tested by stressful circumstances and by spiritual challenges. Recall Genesis 6:9: "This is the account of Noah and his family. Noah was a righteous man, blameless among the people of his time, and he walked faithfully with God." Look at that word *account*. What is the account of your life? "Each of us will give an account of ourselves to God" (Romans 14:12). The world system, cancel culture, and political correctness will try to dismiss and diminish your faith. Stand firm in your faith, and God will use you, as He used Noah in his day.

Noah's faith brought him "favor in the eyes of the LORD" (Genesis 6:8) because he walked with God. God honors a person's faith. We get God's attention when we trust Him. "Without faith it is impossible to please God, because anyone who comes to him must believe he exists and that he rewards those who earnestly seek him" (Hebrews 11:6). Jesus calls everyone to believe in Him. Every person's destiny and eternal destination turn on the axis of the moment he or she believes in Jesus as Savior.

The Future

Noah saved the future. What you build today will carry you tomorrow. Building the Ark represented Noah's faith in action. Everything the Lord commanded him to do regarding the Ark, he did exactly (see Genesis 6:22). The Ark was built by his faith in action. *Your faith determines your future!*

When Noah started building the Ark, the world at that time barely noticed. However, his act of faith saved the world. Noah saved the future of the world, the animals, and humanity.

When You Stand Alone

Noah teaches us the power of influence that one person can have on his or her generation. Noah was only one, but he

The Days of Noah Return

listened to God when others ignored Him. We, too, walk with God in a wicked and violent world. Noah's life serves as an example that we can make a difference. He built the Ark and saved his family and the future of the world. What you build today will carry you tomorrow.

The most important thing is to be in touch with God. God told Noah to build an Ark in order to save his family, and he knew calamity was coming at some point, but God did not give him a time frame. Noah did not know the specifics of what would happen when the floodwaters came. He was told only to get ready for what was coming.

We don't know everything about the future, and God will seldom tell us much about it, because He wants us to live by faith each day and not worry about the future. If you have faith, then you won't worry about the future. Noah is an example to us to act on what we know and not worry about what we don't know. We need to take action today so we are prepared for what will happen tomorrow, and not get taken by surprise.

Just as Noah finished the work of God, we need to complete the work God gives us to do. He gives us the plan, but He requires us to build it. And He expects us to help others along the way. Noah, a preacher of righteousness, must have warned the people about the consequences of their sin and that disaster was at hand. They had an obligation to listen and to obey. "If you are willing and obedient, you will eat the good things of the land" (Isaiah 1:19). But they were not willing and obedient.

My father, who was an engineer, was a man of common sense. I learned from him that when Christians live by the three eternal values of faith, hope, and love, their lives serve as a powerful witness for Jesus even without a word. When I was a teenager, he gave me a poem by Edgar Albert Guest to teach me the power of an exemplary life:

I'd rather see a sermon than hear one any day;
I'd rather one should walk with me than merely tell
   the way.
The eye's a better pupil and more willing than the ear.
Fine counsel is confusing, but example's always
   clear;
And the best of all the preachers are the men who
   live their creeds,
For to see good put in action is what everybody needs.

I soon can learn to do it if you'll let me see it done;
I can watch your hands in action, but your tongue
   too fast may run.
And the lecture you deliver may be very wise and
   true,
But I'd rather get my lessons by observing what
   you do;
For I might misunderstand you and the high advice
   you give,
But there's no misunderstanding how you act and
   how you live.[4]

FIVE

THE SOCIETY OF SODOM

In 1666 a rumor spread through England that the end of the world was coming soon. Certain Bible students may have drawn this conclusion from relating the mark of the Beast to that particular year. As the rumor spread, more and more people, commoner and royalty alike, lived under a sense of impending disaster.

That summer, while Judge Matthew Hale, a man strong in faith, presided over his courtroom, a violent storm arose in western Europe and the British Isles. A lawyer present that day wrote the following description of the event:

> All of the courtroom grew completely black, although it was still mid day. The entire building seemed to shake as thunder shook the walls and bright flashes of lightning momentarily illuminated the room. The people in the courtroom were overcome with fear. And as if by common consent, each person fell to their knees and prayed for mercy, believing that the terrible day of the Lord had finally arrived.[1]

The lawyer noticed, however, that Judge Hale sat unmoved by the event, and continued to take notes of the trial as though nothing out of the ordinary had happened. The lawyer concluded that "Judge Hale's heart was so stayed on God that no surprise (no matter how sudden) could discompose him."[2]

The end of the age and the personal, powerful return of our Lord is a promise of hope, not a prediction of doom.

Another of the intriguing signs Jesus gave of His coming is the return of the days of Sodom and Gomorrah. The destruction of those ancient cities some four thousand years ago is still known today. Interestingly we use the word *sodomy* for the immorality derived from the name of the city because its widespread moral decay is forever embedded in history.

After Jesus compared the last days to the days of Noah, He went on to say:

> "It was the same in the days of Lot. People were eating and drinking, buying and selling, planting and building. But the day Lot left Sodom, fire and sulfur rained down from heaven and destroyed them all. It will be just like this on the day the Son of Man is revealed. On that day no one who is on the housetop, with possessions inside, should go down to get them. Likewise, no one in the field should go back for anything. Remember Lot's wife!"
>
> Luke 17:28–32

Who was Lot? What was going on in Sodom? Why did Jesus refer to Lot's wife? Why is she an important part of Bible prophecy?

The Days of Lot

Lot was the nephew of Abraham who came with him to the Promised Land. Lot knew the promise God gave Abraham of a great land, a great people, and the blessing of the Messiah, through whom all nations would be blessed.

Abraham was Lot's spiritual father and mentor. But their possessions grew to the point that they needed to choose separate places to live.

A Pagan City

Life turns on the axis of big decisions, and Lot faced a big decision. The major decisions we make shape the destiny of our lives.

Lot *looked* at Sodom and was enticed by the "big city lights"—the rich grazing land where he could graze his flocks and herds. He "saw that the whole plain of the Jordan . . . was well watered, like the garden of the LORD" (Genesis 13:10).

He *located* near the city—"Lot . . . pitched his tents near Sodom" (Genesis 13:12)—so he and his family could enjoy the conveniences of the city of Sodom. In our context, they could go into town and shop and eat at fine restaurants and enjoy the night life. Perhaps he had no intention of living in Sodom, but he made the mistake of eventually moving his family into the city.

Once he *lived* in that wicked city, he became enmeshed in the pagan culture.

Our social environment, much more than genetics, tends to be the major determinant of our beliefs and behavior. Lot was no longer under the spiritual guidance of Abraham, the man of faith; and he and his family were surrounded by, and apparently acclimatized to, the immoral and idolatrous culture of Sodom.

A Corrupt City

Genesis 13:13 sums it up: "The people of Sodom were wicked and were sinning greatly against the LORD." *Wicked* is like wicker furniture—twisted out of shape. Their minds and souls were twisted. Note that they sinned greatly against the Lord. All sin is against the Lord and a transgression of the law of God. David prayed, "Against you, you only, have I sinned and done what is evil in your sight" (Psalm 51:4).

Apparently Lot had become a leader in Sodom (see Genesis 19:1), but in name only; he exerted no real influence. Lot's daughters became engaged to ungodly men and began to lose their faith in God as they became part of the pagan culture.

The apostle Peter tells us that Lot, a righteous man, "was distressed" by the filthy lives of lawless men, "for that righteous man, living among them day after day, was tormented in his righteous soul by the lawless deeds he saw and heard" (2 Peter 2:7–8). But Lot became complacent living in Sodom, where his neighbors were corrupt. The place where we live has a profound effect on our attitudes, values, beliefs, and philosophy of life. And later Lot himself actually hesitated to leave.

A City Facing Judgment

The three angels of the Lord who visited Abraham, Lot's uncle, had told him, speaking for God: "The outcry against Sodom and Gomorrah is so great and their sin so grievous that I will go down and see if what they have done is as bad as the outcry that has reached me" (Genesis 18:20–21).

Later two of the angels sent to deliver Lot and his family told him, "We are going to destroy this place. The outcry to the LORD against its people is so great that he has sent us to destroy it."

A Terrifying Night

The Flood in Noah's day and the firestorm of Sodom were natural disasters that became acts of judgment because the people sinned against God and refused to heed the warning. Both disasters could have been avoided if the people had turned to God in repentance and faith. When Jonah warned the wicked city of Nineveh, for example, the king listened and called the city to repentance, and judgment was averted.

Even so, the story of Sodom is a story of grace. God sent two angels, or messengers (the word *angel* means messenger), representing the Gospel of salvation, to tell Lot to get his family out of the city.

The people in Sodom could have left as well, but they refused. The last days will be the same:

> The rest of mankind who were not killed by these plagues *still did not repent* of the work of their hands; they did not stop worshiping demons, and idols of gold, silver, bronze, stone and wood—idols that cannot see or hear or walk. *Nor did they repent* of their murders, their magic arts, their sexual immorality or their thefts.
>
> Revelation 9:20–21, emphasis added

Furthermore:

> The fifth angel poured out his bowl on the throne of the beast, and its kingdom was plunged into darkness. People gnawed their tongues in agony and cursed the God of heaven because of their pains and their sores, but *they refused to repent* of what they had done.
>
> Revelation 16:10–11, emphasis added

Instead of turning to God, these people turned against Him by refusing to repent of their deeds, and cursing Him instead of worshiping Him.

The wicked and violent men of Sodom met the two angels sent to save Lot and his family. But instead of welcoming them, they went to Lot's house as a mob and banged on the door, demanding that Lot turn the two over to them so they could have sex with them. It resembled a scene from the movie *Night of the Living Dead*, with zombies trying to break into the house and kill those hiding there for safety. Lot, his wife, and their two daughters and sons-in-law must have been terrified, wondering when the mob would break through the door.

Lot, lacking commitment and courage, actually offered to give his own daughters to the mob in exchange for the angels. Such an offer by their father was unconscionable. He should have called on the Lord for help and rebuked the men in the name of the Lord. But instead of standing up to them, he tried to placate them. He tried to negotiate with the mob instead of refusing their demands. The climate of Sodom had whittled away at his faith.

When the men of Sodom moved to break down Lot's door, they were struck with instantaneous blindness and were left groping in the darkness.

Here is an interesting lesson: When we reject God's Word, we become spiritually blind to truth and to the Gospel. Jesus said, "The eye is the lamp of the body. . . . If then the light within you is darkness, how great is that darkness!" (Matthew 6:22–23). When people curse God and refuse to repent when they know the truth, it only increases their spiritual blindness.

The Society of Sodom

Lot's Hesitation

The angels told Lot that the city would be destroyed and to get his family out. Lot told his sons-in-law, but they "thought he was joking" (Genesis 19:14). When the sun rose, the angels again urged Lot to flee: "Hurry! Take your wife and your two daughters who are here, or you will be swept away when the city is punished" (Genesis 19:15).

Lot's response at this point in the story is strange: He should have moved with haste, but "he hesitated" (Genesis 19:16). He should have left, but he lingered. He should have been resolved, but he was double-minded between staying and leaving.

We have all been taught that patience is a virtue—and it is. My mother was fond of saying to me, "Fools rush in where angels fear to tread." We have all heard that "good things come to those who wait." There are times, however, when patience is not a virtue. When it is time to flee, don't be patient. Get moving!

> When [Lot] hesitated, the men grasped his hand and the hands of his wife and of his two daughters and led them safely out of the city, for the LORD was merciful to them.
>
> Genesis 19:16

The Lord was merciful to Lot and his family. What a beautiful revelation of the heart of God and His motive to save humanity! "His anger lasts only a moment" (Psalm 30:5) but "his love endures forever" (Psalm 100:5). Even a city facing judgment had an opportunity to receive the mercy of God and be saved. Everyone in the city of Sodom could have been spared, had they responded to God's mercy, but they refused to listen and repent.

One of the angels added this caution to Lot and his family: "Flee for your lives! Don't look back. . . . Flee to the mountains or you will be swept away!" (Genesis 19:17). The message was a warning and a hope. God will always give us a way of escape.

Why did Lot's sons-in-law not listen to him when he warned them? Why did Lot hesitate? Why did he not listen to the angels? Why do we not listen to God?

For at least two reasons.

We don't listen because we don't recognize the messenger. Angels are messengers who look like ordinary men. (The angels in Genesis 19 were also called men.) "Do not forget to show hospitality to strangers, for by so doing some people have shown hospitality to angels without knowing it" (Hebrews 13:2).

The messengers God sends us, through whom He speaks, may be parents, pastors, counselors, or friends. The people in Nazareth were offended at Jesus' teaching because He was the son of Joseph, the carpenter. They did not recognize Him as the Son of God. Consequently Jesus did not perform great miracles there—because of their unbelief. "A prophet is not without honor," He said, "except in his own town" (Mark 6:4).

We don't listen because we don't like the message. The angels told Lot and his family to leave immediately, but they wanted to stay. God's Word demands a prompt reply of *Yes!* "Today, if you hear his voice, do not harden your hearts" (Hebrews 3:7–8).

Scottish theologian William Barclay told the story of three apprentice demons coming to earth to start tempting people. They met with Satan, who questioned their tactics to tempt and destroy mankind.

The first said, "I will tell them there is no God."

Satan responded, "That won't work, since many people know God exists."

The second demon said, "I'll tell them there is no judgment."

Satan replied, "Very few will believe that lie because they know there are consequences to sin."

The third apprentice demon said, "I'll tell them there is no hurry."

Satan said, "You will be very effective in your deception to lead mankind astray."[3]

When God speaks, receive it, believe it, and act on it!

Destruction!

The destruction of Sodom and Gomorrah, which took place at the southeastern shore of the Dead Sea in the time of Abraham, about 1900 BC, is described vividly in Genesis:

> The LORD rained down burning sulfur on Sodom and Gomorrah —from the LORD out of the heavens. Thus he overthrew those cities and the entire plain, destroying all those living in the cities—and also the vegetation in the land.
>
> Genesis 19:24–25

The Promised Land is adjacent to the East Africa Rift zone, a deep break in the earth's crust and one of the most extensive rifts on the earth's surface. Archaeological research suggests that a great earthquake once opened the rift zone, releasing "brimstone" (sulfur) and volatile petroleum gases, which caused a terrible firestorm.

During my first year at a Christian college, a friend and I were invited to a party. In the apartment everyone was talking, eating snacks, and playing loud music. My friend and I noticed a few students drinking beer and doing drugs, but we ignored them. Suddenly there was a loud knock on the door. Two policemen were standing in the doorway. They said they had received a complaint by neighbors of loud music, and they demanded that it be turned down. But they also surveyed the apartment carefully before they left.

My friend and I panicked because a few of the students had drugs.

"Let's get out of here," I said. "Those cops were surveilling this place, and they'll be back in few minutes to do a drug bust."

So we got out of there fast. We knew we were in the wrong place at the wrong time with the wrong people—and judgment was standing at the door!

After one of the angels told Lot and his family to flee to the mountains and not look back, Lot replied:

> "I can't flee to the mountains; this disaster will overtake me, and I'll die. Look, here is a town near enough to run to, and it is small. Let me flee to it—it is very small, isn't it? Then my life will be spared."
>
> Genesis 19:19–20

So they let him go to the town of Zoar (meaning "small"), which was spared. But when the firestorm came, a tragedy occurred: "Lot's wife looked back, and she became a pillar of salt" (Genesis 19:26). She was now safe and secure, but she longed for Sodom. She doubted the word of God. She believed her feelings over the command of the angelic messengers sent from the Lord.

The Society of Sodom

When the Bible says, "She looked back," I believe she longed to return to the comfortable life she had loved in Sodom, where her husband owned substantial flocks and herds and where they probably lived in luxury. I believe Lot's wife had lived for pleasure. And when she looked back, that is when she met her end. Even as Sodom was destroyed by the explosion of brimstone that fell over the plains, Lot's wife was turned into a pillar of salt.

You can visit the salt and mineral deposits that remain by the Dead Sea to this day. The geological evidence of the storm remains. You can still see the massive hills of salt and minerals as the residue of that ancient sulfur storm. I have visited this ancient site.

As the Roman city of Pompeii was being excavated, the body of a woman was found mummified by the volcanic ash of Mount Vesuvius. Her position told a tragic story. Her feet pointed toward the city gate, but her outstretched arms and fingers were straining for something that lay behind her. The treasure for which she was grasping was a bag of pearls. Clovis Chappell writes:

> Though death was hard at her heels, and life was beckoning to her beyond the city gates, she could not shake off their spell. . . . But it was not the eruption of Vesuvius that made her love pearls more than life. It only froze her in this attitude of greed.[4]

"Remember Lot's Wife!"

While Jesus was telling His disciples about His Second Coming and the return of the Sodom society, He made this cryptic statement: "Remember Lot's wife!" (Luke 17:32). Why is this saying of our Lord important to us? In what ways are we to remember her?

Lot's wife is important because of the people Jesus does not tell us to remember. He does not tell us to remember the matriarchs of faith—Sarah, Rebekah, Leah, Rahab, or Ruth. He did not tell us to remember the patriarchs and prophets—Abraham, Isaac, Jacob, Joseph, Moses or David, Jeremiah or Isaiah. Instead He said, "Remember Lot's wife!"

Lot's wife is important because of the One who mentioned her. It was Jesus, the Prince of Peace, who taught that the greatest commandment is love, who was meek and humble of heart—yet He said, "Remember Lot's wife!"

Lot's wife is important because of those to whom Jesus was talking. He did not make this statement to casual onlookers, or to the Pharisees, or to a crowd looking for a miracle, but to His disciples who carried on His ministry. He said, "Remember Lot's wife!"

Jesus' caution to us is important because of the subject He was discussing—His Second Coming. Our Lord told us to be ready, watchful, and faithful in view of His return. He is the One who said, "Remember Lot's wife!"

Why does Jesus want us to remember Lot's wife? Her life could have been a testimony. Sadly she made her life a tragedy. It is a tragedy when a person gives up salvation for Sodom!

What life lessons can we learn from her failure that will keep us from making the same mistakes?

She Lacked Faith

Remember Lot's wife because she was surrounded by faith but had no faith. She was part of a family of faith led by

Abraham, her husband's uncle, the man of faith. She inherited faith but did not integrate it into her life.

It is a great privilege to grow up in a Christian family, or to have Christian friends, but each person must come to Christ. You cannot depend on other people's faith in God. You must experience Jesus and believe in Him personally. Jesus says to every person, "Whoever believes in Me has eternal life" (see John 3:15). You must believe in Jesus for yourself.

The angels had to drag Lot and his family out of Sodom because they were out of tune spiritually with God.

Often Christians with good intentions try to drag people to Christ. We want the best for people, so we put spiritual pressure on family and friends. We need to guide others to Jesus but not pressure them. We need to trust the power of the Gospel we share and the Person of the Holy Spirit to do the work of salvation.

Nobody, not even an angel of God, can do it for you. You must make up your own mind about Jesus. Daniel made up his mind when exiled to Babylon that he would follow God, not that culture. "Daniel resolved not to defile himself" (Daniel 1:8). While in prison, Paul the apostle wrote, "I know whom I have believed" (2 Timothy 1:12). Make up your mind about Jesus and believe in Him. Nobody, not even an angel of God, can do it for you. You must decide for yourself the life you want to live, the faith you want to believe, and the destiny you want to experience.

She Held on to the World

Remember Lot's wife because she held on to a world that had no lasting value. When she looked back at Sodom, she longed for the place she loved, which was undergoing destruction and judgment, instead of hurrying away from that city and walking toward God's new season for her and her family. The angels were leading her and her family to salvation—but she looked back.

What a tragedy! This present world is temporary; it has no lasting value. "Do not love the world or anything in the world. . . . The world and its desires pass away, but whoever does the will of God lives forever" (1 John 2:15, 17). Jesus said, "Store up for yourselves treasures in heaven" (Matthew 6:20). As believers "we fix our eyes not on what is seen, but on what is unseen, since what is seen is temporary, but what is unseen is eternal" (2 Corinthians 4:18). We tend to hold on to the things we need to let go of, and let go of the things we need to hold on to.

"For here we do not have an enduring city, but we are looking for the city that is to come" (Hebrews 13:14). Moses "chose to be mistreated along with the people of God rather than to enjoy the fleeting pleasures of sin. He regarded disgrace for the sake of Christ as of greater value than the treasures of Egypt, because he was looking ahead to his reward" (Hebrews 11:25–26). Abraham became a wealthy and influential man in Canaan, but in a temporal world, he kept an eternal perspective. "He was looking forward to the city with foundations, whose architect and builder is God" (Hebrews 11:10).

Lot's wife, on the other hand, chose a city under judgment and lost everything. She chose judgment instead of justification.

This world has no lasting value for us. All its fame, fortune, power, and pleasure never last. "We are receiving a kingdom that cannot be shaken!" (Hebrews 12:28). As a Christian, you have been given "an inheritance that can never perish, spoil or fade . . . kept in heaven for you" (1 Peter 1:4).

She Forfeited God's Grace

Remember Lot's wife because she forfeited the grace God offered her. Jonah said, "Those who cling to worthless idols forfeit the grace that could be theirs" (Jonah 2:8 NIV1984). Every person will face God and give an account for how he or she has responded to God's grace. "It is appointed for men to die once, but after this the judgment" (Hebrews 9:27 NKJV). *Judgment* means to be evaluated and to give an account: "We will all stand before God's judgment seat. . . . So then, each of us will give an account of ourselves to God" (Romans 14:10, 12).

The only way to be ready for that final exam of life is to experience the saving grace of God that frees us from judgment. When you accept Christ as Savior, who died in your place, you are forgiven of all your sin and transgressions. God sees you clothed in the righteousness of Christ. "God made him [Jesus] who had no sin to be sin for us, so that in him we might become the righteousness of God" (2 Corinthians 5:21). As a result, "There is now no condemnation for those who are in Christ Jesus" (Romans 8:1). No guilty verdict! "We will have confidence on the day of judgment" (1 John 4:17).

On the cross Jesus took our judgment and paid our debt. We are free in Him from judgment! "Since we have now been justified [declared righteous] by his blood, how much more shall we be saved from God's wrath through him!" (Romans 5:9).

Receive the grace of God afforded and freely offered to you.

She Believed Good Times Would Last

Remember Lot's wife because she believed that good times would last. At times our lives seem perfect. Everything comes together for us. We are happy, content, and peaceful. Our relationships are drama-free. Our bank account is good. Our health is strong. Our job is fulfilling. Our hopes are high. But life moves in seasons. It is a journey with mountains and valleys, calm seas and raging storms, successes and failures.

Lot's wife lived in the lap of luxury. She found her comfort zone in Sodom and had no reason to assume the good times would not last—but they never do.

Lot's wife is like many today who do not believe in the return of Christ, the rise of the Antichrist, and the Great Tribulation coming on this world, all foretold in the Word of God. That is why Jesus said the attitudes of the people in Sodom describe the world before His return. They do not believe that God will bring an end to the world as we know it. But He will.

The end is just the beginning, however, for God will make "a new heaven and a new earth, where righteousness dwells" (2 Peter 3:13).

Years ago I was visiting a successful and wealthy man who was given a bleak prognosis. He told me he could not believe this was happening to him. Recently retired, with the next season planned, he thought the good times would continue. Now he was filled with fear and wanted to talk about his relationship with God. Suddenly the good life meant little to him. Facing eternity, he was ready to hear the best news any of us will hear—that Jesus Christ came to give us eternal life. I prayed with him, and he found peace with God.

She Looked Back Instead of Forward

Remember Lot's wife because she looked back instead of looking forward. You may be tempted by the allure of this world to go back to your old life, your old habits, or your old relationships. Be on your guard—"for everything in the world—the lust of the flesh, the lust of the eyes, and the pride of life—comes not from the Father but from the world" (1 John 2:16).

We can also be misled spiritually away from Christ. Paul wrote, "I am afraid that just as Eve was deceived by the serpent's cunning, your minds may somehow be led astray from your sincere and pure devotion to Christ" (2 Corinthians 11:3). Jesus told us that many false prophets and false messiahs would arise in the last days and "deceive many" (Matthew 24:5). Paul continued, "Such people are false apostles, deceitful workers, masquerading as apostles of Christ. And no wonder, for Satan himself masquerades as an angel of light" (2 Corinthians 11:13–14).

Daniel Webster Whittle was a nineteenth-century hymnwriter and associate of evangelist Dwight L. Moody, who wrote the lyrics to some two hundred songs, including "I Know Whom I Have Believed" and "Showers of Blessing." While he was serving in the Civil War, a nurse asked him to pray for a young soldier near death. Whittle was not even a Christian at the time, but she thought he was because he carried a Bible and read it all the time.

He felt it was wrong to pray for the soldier since he was not a Christian, but he knelt to pray. And when he did, the Holy Spirit moved on his heart, and he asked Christ to forgive him of his sins. When he finished praying, the soldier had passed peacefully into eternity.

The book *Twice-Born Men* features the account of Whittle's conversion and his awe of the grace of God, which had saved him and through which he had led the soldier to Christ.[5]

Give your heart fully to Jesus Christ. Commit yourself to Him with a sincere and pure devotion. Make a clean break with the world and move on toward your divine destiny. Don't look back. Look forward to the city with foundations and keep pressing on for the high calling of God.

Remember Lot's wife!

SIX

THE COMING GLOBAL ORDER

The history of the world is marked by great empires that now lie in obscurity. Jesus foretold a time of Tribulation coming to the whole world that will be unequaled by any other time in history. At the heart of the Great Tribulation is the institution of a new global order led by the Antichrist. Jesus predicted it this way:

> "There will be great distress, unequaled from the beginning of the world until now—and never to be equaled again. If those days had not been cut short, no one would survive, but for the sake of the elect those days will be shortened. . . . Immediately after the distress of those days 'the sun will be darkened, and the moon will not give its light; the stars will fall from the sky, and the heavenly bodies will be shaken.' Then will appear the sign of the Son of Man in heaven. And then all the peoples of the earth will mourn when they see

the Son of Man coming on the clouds of heaven, with power and great glory."

Matthew 24:21–22, 29–30

This time of unequaled distress, the Great Tribulation, sets the stage for the rise of the Antichrist and the promise of a global order of world peace.

Bertrand Russell, atheist, social activist, and opponent of the Christian faith, wrote about the coming global order:

I believe that, owing to men's folly, a world-government will only be established by force, and will therefore be at first cruel and despotic. But I believe that it is necessary for the preservation of a scientific civilization, and that, if once realized, it will gradually give rise to the other conditions of a tolerable existence.[1]

The Bible refers to this period as the time of Jacob's trouble (see Jeremiah 30:6–7), the day of "indignation" (Isaiah 26:20 NKJV), and Daniel's seventy weeks (see Daniel 9:24–27). Many scholars believe the Great Tribulation will last for seven years, a time frame based on Daniel's prophecy concerning seventy weeks. This future period will be filled with such trouble that, in Jesus' words, "People will faint from terror, apprehensive of what is coming on the world, for the heavenly bodies will be shaken" (Luke 21:26).

People today are already apprehensive about the future. The global pandemic, changing politics, economic instability, and persistent wars generate widespread panic. The Antichrist will build his global empire; the mark of the Beast will govern economics; persecution will increase against those who worship God; and it will end at Armageddon, when Christ returns.

The archangel Gabriel told Daniel:

"Know and understand this: From the time the word goes out to restore and rebuild Jerusalem until the Anointed One, the ruler, comes, there will be seven 'sevens,' and sixty-two 'sevens.' It will be rebuilt with streets and a trench, but in times of trouble. After the sixty-two 'sevens,' the Anointed One will be put to death and will have nothing. The people of the ruler who will come will destroy the city and the sanctuary. The end will come like a flood: War will continue until the end, and desolations have been decreed. He will confirm a covenant with many for one 'seven.' In the middle of the 'seven' he will put an end to sacrifice and offering. And at the temple he will set up an abomination that causes desolation, until the end that is decreed is poured out on him."

Daniel 9:25–27

Let's look more closely at Daniel's prophecy.

Prophetic Weeks

The mysterious seventy weeks of Daniel's prophecy provide the time frame of seven years: "Seventy 'sevens' are decreed for your people [Israel] and your holy city [Jerusalem]" (Daniel 9:24). This vision of seventy "sevens," or weeks, refers to a period of 490 years of history. (One week represents seven years, and seven times seventy equals 490 years.) The seventy weeks are about Jesus' coming—first as Suffering Servant, and then, at the end of the age, as conquering King. He came first to Bethlehem to redeem, but He will return the second time to reign.

Daniel's vision gives six reasons for the seventy prophetic weeks: "to finish transgression, to put an end to sin, to atone for wickedness, to bring in everlasting righteousness, to seal up vision and prophecy and to anoint the Most Holy Place" (Daniel 9:24).

The seventy weeks consists of three sections.

The first seven weeks constitute 49 years for the rebuilding of Jerusalem under Zerubbabel, governor of Judah after the remnant returned from Babylonian captivity.

Then there are 62 sevens, equaling 434 years, from the decree to rebuild the Temple until the crucifixion of Jesus, when "the Anointed One will be put to death and will have nothing" (verse 26). The prophetic accuracy of the time frame of Jesus' coming into the world as Messiah—given more than five hundred years before Jesus lived—is an undeniable testimony to the divine inspiration of Scripture.

Finally, the one remaining week of seven years is viewed as the seven-year Great Tribulation, which will end with Christ's return at the battle of Armageddon. In this final week of the Tribulation period, Israel is the focal point of God's activity. That is why the angel tells Daniel that "seventy 'sevens' are decreed for your people [Israel] and your holy city [Jerusalem]" (Daniel 9:24). Today Israel is the focal point of the world in the Middle East. The angel also describes the Antichrist in this passage. He is called "the ruler who will come" (verse 26) who will invade Jerusalem and who will meet his end at Armageddon—in Daniel's prophecy, "until the end that is decreed is poured out on him" (verse 27).

Specific world conditions will emerge during the Tribulation period and the coming Antichrist kingdom. Global economy, religious intolerance, and fascist politics will be

The Coming Global Order

the order of the day when the Antichrist tries to unite the world under his control. While he will never gain control of the whole world, he will gain control of many nations. The world will suffer from the Antichrist's tyranny during the Great Tribulation.

Have you noticed how many politicians are advocating a global government? The United Nations, international law, the World Health Organization, limits to national sovereignty, global redistribution of wealth, global currency—these are only a few of the signs of world government in the making.

Many politicians, corporate executives, and social activists believe naïvely that globalism and big government are the answers to the needs of the world. But every totalitarian government and kingdom of the past has perished over time, and so will the kingdom of the Antichrist when Jesus returns in power and glory to bring the only global government we need—the Kingdom of God!

World Religion

The Antichrist will be assisted by the false prophet, who will work to promote the Antichrist's agenda in the worst possible blend of the state and religion. The apostle John described the false prophet as "a second beast, coming out of the earth" (Revelation 13:11). He will manipulate people to worship and honor the Antichrist as a god.

Roman emperors starting with Julius Caesar were viewed as divine. Citizens were required to pledge their allegiance with the oath "Caesar is Lord," while Christians refused to bow the knee to a statue of the emperor. Their confession and ours is still "Jesus is Lord!"

When Communism took over in China, Russia, and Cuba, the government recognized and allowed only state churches. Government undercover agents visit these churches and track the worshipers to prevent political dissent or unapproved doctrine from being taught or preached.

During the 2020 presidential election in the U.S., the government tracked media sites and social media posts to limit free speech about the election and to note people's responses to the global pandemic. After the election, I preached a sermon entitled "Election Results"—a title that was flagged on social media with a caution. My sermon had nothing to do with the presidential election, however, but rather the doctrine of election. The apostle Peter, for example, wrote

> to God's elect, exiles scattered throughout the provinces . . . who have been chosen according to the foreknowledge of God the Father, through the sanctifying work of the Spirit, to be obedient to Jesus Christ and sprinkled with his blood.
>
> 1 Peter 1:1–2

I used the recent election as a focal point to preach about divine election and foreknowledge and our free will to believe in Jesus. The fact is, people are free to think and say what they believe, according to the First Amendment of the U.S. Constitution, which guarantees, among other rights, "the freedom of speech." But some politicians, although they have taken a solemn oath to uphold the Constitution, violate this right. Some media companies are influenced by pressure from the government to monitor and suppress people's political views. Some public school boards refuse to inform parents of inappropriate materials being taught to their children.

The Coming Global Order

These are examples of the greater government control and persecution that will characterize the global government in the last days.

Global Economics

The Antichrist kingdom will control economics and establish a universal ID system to track everyone. The mark of the Beast, expressed by the numerical value 666, will be placed on either the forehand or the forehead of those loyal to the Antichrist, and without it no one can conduct financial transactions. The mark is not just a means to conduct financial transactions but a sign of loyalty to the Antichrist. The false prophet

> forced all people, great and small, rich and poor, free and slave, to receive a mark on their right hands or on their foreheads, so that they could not buy or sell unless they had the mark, which is the name of the beast or the number of its name. This calls for wisdom. Let the person who has insight calculate the number of the beast, for it is the number of a man. That number is 666.
>
> Revelation 13:16–18

The number 666 may be called the number of a man, since man was created on the sixth day of creation (see Genesis 1:26–31).

The stage is already set. The technology is here. Some governments already track deposits and withdrawals in bank accounts over certain amounts. Computers and smartphones track data, search histories, political persuasions, religious affiliations, and personal contacts of families and friends. Computer chips are already being implanted into the hand for identification and financial transactions. Children could have a chip placed in them at birth so they can be traced if they are ever abducted. Credit card and ATM fraud and robbery would virtually disappear if chips were used instead of bank cards.

I am not saying that computer chips embedded in a person's hand is necessarily the mark of the Beast. But I am saying that such technology makes it possible for global control of every person by a diabolical dictator like the Antichrist.

The World Bank and International Monetary Fund (IMF), both established in 1944 and based in Washington, D.C., work in tandem to provide loans, especially to developing countries, to promote economic growth and economic stability and alleviate poverty. Again, I am not suggesting there is anything wrong with these financial institutions. But global economic control under the wrong leadership poses a great threat to the world and to the independence and national sovereignty of the nations of the world.

The mark of the Beast shows the danger of economic control. Such control already exists in Islamic states and Communist nations. Socialism and Communism are the greatest threats to the economic freedom and prosperity of thriving nations, which have economies based on personal responsibility, a strong work ethic, and free-market capitalism, allowing people to excel in life.

Socialism and Communism are systems of economic control. Politicians and university professors anywhere in the world who advocate Marxism are a dangerous threat to freedom. Karl Marx, author with Friedrich Engels of *The Communist Manifesto*, described socialism as the transition between capitalism and Communism.

Liberation theology blends the Gospel of Jesus Christ with Marxism, resulting in a distortion of true justice. Some have suggested that the Church after Pentecost practiced socialism, but nothing could be further from the truth:

> All the believers were one in heart and mind. No one claimed that any of their possessions was their own, but they *shared* everything they had. With great power the apostles continued to testify to the resurrection of the Lord Jesus. And God's grace was so powerfully at work in them all that there were no needy persons among them.
>
> Acts 4:32–34, emphasis added

The believers freely shared what they had with each other, but there is a big difference sharing freely and forced socialism. Grace produces generosity.

Increased Persecution

Persecution is the greatest injustice ever afflicted on God's people by political and religious tyrants. Those who follow Jesus during the Tribulation will suffer great persecution. People will worship underground to escape the Antichrist system, as they do today in nations that suppress religious freedom. The history of the Church has been marked by persecution. The same is true for the nation of Israel.

John the apostle saw a vision of "a mystery: Babylon the Great," the Antichrist religious system, "drunk with the blood of God's holy people, the blood of those who bore testimony to Jesus" (Revelation 17:5–6). Jesus said, "If the world hates you, keep in mind that it hated me first" (John 15:18). Paul reminded us, "Everyone who wants to live a godly life in Christ Jesus will be persecuted, while evildoers and impostors will go from bad to worse, deceiving and being deceived" (2 Timothy 3:12–13).

As we noted in chapter 1, John the Revelator saw the souls of Christian martyrs throughout history, crying out to God for justice:

> When [the Lamb] opened the fifth seal, I saw under the altar the souls of those who had been slain because of the word of God and the testimony they had maintained. They called out in a loud voice, "How long, Sovereign Lord, holy and true, until you judge the inhabitants of the earth and avenge our blood?" Then each of them was given a white robe, and they were told to wait a little longer, until the full number of their fellow servants, their brothers and sisters, were killed just as they had been.
>
> Revelation 6:9–11

The word *testimony* is from the Greek word *martyr*. A martyr is a faithful witness of Jesus. The group Open Doors USA estimates that 317 million Christians last year lived in countries where persecution was significant. Approximately 4,998 Christians were murdered, more than 4,000 were detained or imprisoned, and almost 15,000 churches and Christian properties were attacked.[2]

While persecution is real and tragic, it is no threat to the Gospel of Christ and to faithful believers who stand firm to the end. Even though the body perishes, the soul is saved eternally in heaven. As Christians, we are instructed to remember, honor, and pray for fellow believers who suffer persecution.

The book of Hebrews was written during the outbreak of Roman persecution, when the government was seizing the property of believers, closing their businesses, and imprisoning and killing them. The author wrote to encourage them to stand fast:

> Remember those earlier days after you had received the light, when you endured in a great conflict full of suffering. Sometimes you were publicly exposed to insult and persecution; at other times you stood side by side with those who were so treated. You suffered along with those in prison and joyfully accepted the confiscation of your property, because you knew that you yourselves had better and lasting possessions. So do not throw away your confidence; it will be richly rewarded.
>
> Hebrews 10:32–35

We are given this challenge: "Continue to remember those in prison as if you were together with them in prison, and those who are mistreated as if you yourselves were suffering" (Hebrews 13:3).

Motivated by this challenge, I have preached the Gospel in most of the state and federal prisons in Georgia. How much more concerned should we be for Christians imprisoned for their faith in Christ around the world? In the parable of the sheep and the goats, describing the final judgment, Jesus said: "I was in prison and you came to visit me" (Matthew 25:36). Then He gave the disciples the meaning of His statement: "Truly I tell you, whatever you did for one of the least of these brothers and sisters of mine, you did for me" (verse 40).

The book of Hebrews does not bear the name of an apostle or a destination for the letter. Scholars have postulated that it was authored by either Paul or Apollos, an associate of Paul. The apostle's name was probably omitted, along with the name of the congregation being addressed, to protect the identity of the author and the recipients from the Roman government.

This is also why John the apostle called himself "the elder," and the congregation to whom he wrote as "the lady chosen by God and . . . her children, whom I love in the truth" (2 John 1)—to protect their identity. The term *the lady* probably correlates the Church to the Bride of Christ.

Believers privileged to live in a free democratic nation know little of this kind of tyranny, but many believers throughout history, right up to the present time, have followed Christ at great cost and with great courage.

A new rise of anti-Christian persecution and anti-Semitism challenges God's people. Certain politicians and media personalities attack believers with terms like *Christian nationalism*. Some are even church members, hiding behind the cloak of the Church while promoting anti-Christian views. Paul the apostle said about such people that "both their minds and consciences are corrupted. They claim to know God, but by their actions they deny him" (Titus 1:15–16). Profession and practice go hand in hand. When we live out our faith in daily life, we become living witnesses. But "faith without works is dead" (James 2:26 NKJV).

False doctrine starts first inside the Church. "The Spirit clearly says that in later times some will abandon the faith and follow deceiving spirits and things taught by demons" (1 Timothy 4:1). Tragically some Christian denominations and organizations have abandoned the faith and no longer teach about God as Creator; the divinity, atoning death, and bodily resurrection of Jesus; the inspiration of Scripture; the sanctity of human life; the creation of only two sexes, male and female; the exclusivity of marriage as a covenant between a man and a woman; and the sanctity of sexual love within the marriage covenant. The false church persecutes true Christians in the same manner that some of the religious leaders in the first century rejected Jesus instead of receiving Him as the Messiah and Savior of the world.

Divine Accountability

God holds humanity accountable for our actions. His judgment will be unleashed on the Antichrist and his followers, reaching its zenith at the battle of Armageddon and the Second Coming of Christ.

John described the judgment in two series of symbols: seven trumpets, followed by seven bowls of God's wrath.

First, seven trumpets will sound and unleash such things on earth as hail and fire falling from heaven, seas turning to blood like the Egyptian plagues, the sun being darkened, the moon turning to blood, the hosts of Christian martyrs crying for justice, and stars falling from the sky. The sixth trumpet describes an army of two hundred million soldiers marching across the Euphrates River toward Armageddon (see Revelation 8:6–9:16).

Then seven bowls of wrath are poured out on the earth. They are similar in nature to the seven trumpet judgments, with greater intensity. When the sixth bowl of wrath is poured out, the Euphrates River dries up to prepare the way for the kings of the East. Demonic spirits "go out to the kings of the whole world, to gather them for the battle on the great day of God Almighty" (Revelation 16:14). Where does this battle happen? "They gathered the kings together to the place that in Hebrew is called Armageddon" (verse 16). We will look at this in greater detail in chapters 8 and 9.

Judgment for every person is real. "We must all appear before the judgment seat of Christ, so that each of us may receive what is due us for the things done while in the body, whether good or bad" (2 Corinthians 5:10). Life on earth will end in eternity. Hebrews teaches that "people are destined to die once, and after that to face judgment" (Hebrews 9:27).

What sobering words! Are you ready to face the judgment of God knowing that you are saved from your sins through your faith in Jesus Christ? "Whoever lives in love lives in God, and God in them. This is how love is made complete among us so that we will have confidence on the day of judgment: In this world we are like Jesus" (1 John 4:16–17). You can be confident on Judgment Day.

Judgment is certain, not only for individuals but for nations, corrupt politicians, and diabolical dictators:

> The wicked go down to the realm of the dead, all the nations that forget God. But God will never forget the needy; the hope of the afflicted will never perish. Arise, Lord, do not let mortals triumph; let the nations be judged in your presence. Strike them with terror, Lord; let the nations know they are only mortal.
>
> Psalm 9:17–20

But no nation is hopeless. Its leaders and people have the opportunity to repent of sin, turn to God, and put their faith in Him.

When Jonah preached the word of God to the wicked city of Nineveh, revival transpired:

The Coming Global Order

The Ninevites believed God. A fast was proclaimed, and all of them, from the greatest to the least, put on sackcloth. When Jonah's warning reached the king of Nineveh, he rose from his throne, took off his royal robes, covered himself with sackcloth and sat down in the dust.

Jonah 3:5–6

The repentance urged by the king of that city brought revival, and God changed course: "When God saw what they did and how they turned from their evil ways, he relented and did not bring on them the destruction he had threatened" (verse 10).

Once again, after the city of Jerusalem and its leaders crucified Jesus, rejecting the Savior, Peter and the apostles preached the Gospel of the risen Lord Jesus on the Day of Pentecost and exhorted them to repent:

"Repent and be baptized, every one of you, in the name of Jesus Christ for the forgiveness of your sins. And you will receive the gift of the Holy Spirit." . . . With many other words he warned them; and he pleaded with them, "Save yourselves from this corrupt generation." Those who accepted his message were baptized, and about three thousand were added to their number that day.

Acts 2:38, 40–41

God's final judgment on the world is described in the book of Revelation. Seven bowls of God's wrath will be poured out onto the earth: "The seventh angel poured out his bowl into the air, and out of the temple came a loud voice from the throne, saying, 'It is done!'" (Revelation 16:17). "It is done" is the same shout of victory Jesus gave from the cross when

He said, "It is finished!" God will finish in Revelation what He began in Genesis.

Let Revival Come!

The Great Awakening was a period in Church history during the 1700s and 1800s that brought revival to America. The modern missionary movement began as the Church was re-invigorated to fulfill the Great Commission. The Tribulation period will likewise see a great awakening when the Holy Spirit does a new work in the world: "In the last days, God says, I will pour out my Spirit on all people" (Acts 2:17).

The Great Tribulation constitutes the end of this present age and the beginning of the age to come, when Christ reigns as Lord:

> [God] raised Christ from the dead and seated him at his right hand in the heavenly realms, far above all rule and authority, power and dominion, and every name that is invoked, not only in the present age but also in the one to come.
>
> Ephesians 1:20–21

The best is yet to come! Spiritual awakening will take place in the world as the Gospel of Christ is proclaimed during the Tribulation.

The Rapture of the Church may serve as a prophetic sign to the world for people to put their hope in Christ. It may be one of God's final signs—one of epic proportions!—to wake people up and bring them to faith and repentance before the end of days.

John the apostle saw a vision of evangelism during the Tribulation:

The Coming Global Order

Then I saw another angel flying in midair, and he had the eternal gospel to proclaim to those who live on the earth—to every nation, tribe, language and people. He said in a loud voice, "Fear God and give him glory, *because the hour of his judgment has come.*"

Revelation 14:6–7, emphasis added

You see, the Gospel is preached around the world even when the hour of God's judgment comes. But the tragedy of the Tribulation is that many will reject the Gospel of Christ, by which they can be saved:

The rest of mankind who were not killed by these plagues still did not repent of the work of their hands; they did not stop worshiping demons, and idols of gold, silver, bronze, stone and wood—idols that cannot see or hear or walk. Nor did they repent of their murders, their magic arts, their sexual immorality or their thefts.

Revelation 9:20–21

Instead of turning to God to save them, "they cursed God" (Revelation 16:21).

God's judgments and the natural consequences of our sins are intended to lead us to faith and repentance. "Godly sorrow brings repentance that leads to salvation" (2 Corinthians 7:10). God takes no pleasure in judgment. As we saw in the last chapter with Lot and his family, God delights to show mercy: "His anger lasts only a moment" (Psalm 30:5) but "his love endures forever" (Psalm 100:5). The Tribulation judgments are meant not to ruin but to redeem humanity.

But some people today are like Pharaoh, who refused God's repeated commands to let His people go and hardened his heart against God. So God sent plagues to Egypt as signs of His presence and power, calling Pharaoh to repent.

God did not have to send Moses. He did not have to give Pharaoh ten chances to obey with the ten plagues. God is not required to wait for man's repentance. He could have destroyed Pharaoh and Egypt with the strike of His mighty hand. But He is patient and loving, and gave Pharaoh repeated chances to free the Hebrew slaves. At any point Pharaoh could have obeyed God's command through the prophet Moses and stood as a hero of faith. But Pharaoh chose the plagues. He could have ended them at any moment, but he refused to obey God.

How many miracles of judgment did Pharaoh need to see in order to believe and obey? It did not matter how many miracles he saw. He had hardened his heart toward God. The final blow on the night of the Passover, when God struck down all the firstborn of Egypt, left Pharaoh no other option but to free the slaves. Even then he chased after them—and God destroyed his entire army in the waters of the Red Sea.

During the Tribulation people will harden their hearts toward God and the Gospel of Christ. They will choose ruin instead of redemption, suffering instead of salvation, and judgment instead of joy.

C. S. Lewis wrote in *The Great Divorce*: "There are only two kinds of people in the end: those who say to God, 'Thy will be done,' and those to whom God says, in the end, 'Thy will be done.' All that are in hell choose it."[3]

Timeless Truths

Biblical prophecy about the Great Tribulation gives us timeless truths that speak to our lives today. What do we learn? Here are just a few truths.

116

Receive Christ Today

Jesus proclaimed, "The kingdom of God has come near. Repent and believe the good news!" (Mark 1:15). Paul wrote, "Now is the time of God's favor, now is the day of salvation" (2 Corinthians 6:2).

When we repent of our sins and admit we are wrong, then God forgives us and saves us.

Rest in Your Salvation

While the subject of God's judgment is uncomfortable, it reminds us that Jesus took our judgment on the cross, so we don't have to face judgment. "Since we have now been justified by his blood, how much more shall we be saved from God's wrath through him!" (Roman 5:9). "God did not appoint us to suffer wrath but to receive salvation through our Lord Jesus Christ" (1 Thessalonians 5:9).

Finally, "We will have confidence on the day of judgment" (1 John 4:17). We will hear Jesus say to us, "Well done, good and faithful servant!" (Matthew 25:21). The psalmist David spoke of "the joy of your salvation" (Psalm 51:12). During his final days on earth, Paul the apostle wrote: "There is in store for me the crown of righteousness, which the Lord, the righteous Judge, will award to me on that day—and not only to me, but also to all who have longed for his appearing" (2 Timothy 4:8).

Rejoice in God's Providence

The world looks as if it is falling apart, but God holds it and us in the palm of His hand! Moses said, "The eternal God is your refuge, and underneath are the everlasting arms" (Deuteronomy 33:27). Moses pronounced these words over Israel shortly before he died.

History may look as if evil will triumph and the Antichrist will win the day, but Jesus will return and defeat him. God will complete His plan for the world as He "works out everything in conformity with the purpose of his will" (Ephesians 1:11). In the same way, God will also work out everything "for the good of those who love him, who have been called according to his purpose" (Romans 8:28).

The book of Revelation informs us that God will complete His plan for the world. "In the days when the seventh angel is about to sound his trumpet, the mystery of God will be accomplished, just as he announced to his servants the prophets" (Revelation 10:7). While we live in a world of conflict, we must remember that God is in control. As the psalmist David proclaimed in praise, "His kingdom rules over all" (Psalm 103:19).

When Abraham Lincoln was assassinated, the nation went into mourning. There was confusion, despair, and hopelessness. In New York City a crowd gathered to mourn the loss of their great leader and to express concern about the future. Suddenly a man climbed the stairs of a building where he could look out over the crowd, and he shouted, "The Lord reigns over Washington!" The people grew silent as the meaning of his words reassured them. Slowly they began to disperse and go about their business.[4]

As a pastor, I recall the Sunday morning following the tragic day of the 9/11 terrorist attacks. What reassurance could I give the people of God? My mind went immediately to the words of Psalm 46 as I prepared my sermon: "Be still, and know that I am God; I will be exalted among the nations, I will be exalted in the earth" (Psalm 46:10). I could reassure the people that in the face of world chaos, "Our God reigns!"

SEVEN

ANTICHRIST ARISING

I stopped by a restaurant specializing in fine Southern cooking to pick up a meal for takeout. Standing in the checkout line behind me was a man holding a container of collard greens.

"I'm a farmer," he said, "and these collard greens cost $22. Do you know what they should cost?"

"No," I replied. "I grew up in the city. I don't know anything about farming."

"Well, they should cost about five dollars. What's wrong with America? This isn't the America I knew forty years ago."

I told him that times change.

"But what's going wrong with our country?" he insisted.

Other people seemed to be eavesdropping, listening for my reply.

"It all boils down to leadership," I said. "High inflation is the result of poor leadership and bad fiscal policy. Think of it—politicians are the only group of people who ask for a job by promising to make things better. Then, when their policies make things worse, they blame others. None of us gets to do that in our jobs. We have to take responsibility for the results of our decisions and actions. If we do a bad job, we get fired. But politicians get to stay in office. So it all boils down to leadership. Real change starts at the top."

It is often said that everything rises and falls on leadership. Today the world is looking for leadership. We face a leadership crisis. "When the righteous are in authority, the people rejoice; but when a wicked man rules, the people groan" (Proverbs 29:2 NKJV).

The global crisis of the last days will open the door for a leader to come on the scene promising the world peace and prosperity. The Bible calls this end-times leader "the antichrist" (1 John 2:18), "the man of lawlessness" (2 Thessalonians 2:3), and the "beast coming out of the sea" (Revelation 13:1).

What does the Bible teach about the coming Antichrist? John the apostle wrote:

> This is the last hour; and as you have heard that the antichrist is coming, even now many antichrists have come. . . .
>
> Do not believe every spirit, but test the spirits to see whether they are from God. . . . This is how you can recognize the Spirit of God: Every spirit that acknowledges that Jesus Christ has come in the flesh is from God, but every spirit that does not acknowledge Jesus is not from God. This is the spirit of the antichrist, which you have heard is coming and even now is already in the world. You, dear children, are from God and have overcome them, because the one who is in you is greater than the one who is in the world.
>
> 1 John 2:18; 4:1–4, emphasis added

Antichrist Arising

John uses the term *antichrist* in three ways: "the anti-christ," "many antichrists," and "the spirit of the antichrist." Something may not be Christian, but it is not necessarily anti-Christian. *Anti* means to oppose something and it means to replace something.

The antichrist spirit at work in the world today will eventually set the stage for the person of the Antichrist. His power in the last days will extend to political control, religious persecution, and economic oppression.

The spirit of antichrist is seen in totalitarian governments. The tyranny of ancient empires and dictators, Communist regimes, and Islamic law—all share these three traits in common. First, they control the government and refuse free elections, free speech, and government of the people, by the people, and for the people. Second, they persecute every religious and non-religious view—including Jewish people and Christians—that does not conform to their ideology. And finally, they control economics by stringent regulations and excessive taxes to limit the flow of money in society.

Corruption in government always increases poverty, lowers the standard of living, and redistributes wealth unfairly so it flows into the government rather than to the people. In nations that offer more and more social programs, the poor are getting poorer. Socialist politicians offer words, not wealth, and promises, not paychecks. Totalitarian governments champion the sovereignty of the state with no regard for individuals or families.

Antichrists at Large

John the apostle pointed out that throughout history, "many antichrists have come." The Antichrist is the last of a series of many antichrists at large who have appeared, such as the Egyptian pharaohs, Roman emperors, Communist dictators, African warlords and dictators, Islamic ayatollahs, and modern-day globalists.

Globalism is contrary to God's will. God dispersed people at the Tower of Babel, their first attempt at global government, because mankind is too sinful for a global government, which always results in tyranny. God confused the languages and scattered the people so they could not organize a social structure opposed to His will:

> The LORD scattered them from there over all the earth, and they stopped building the city. That is why it was called Babel—because there the LORD confused the language of the whole world. From there the LORD scattered them over the face of the whole earth.
>
> Genesis 11:8–9

English historian Lord Acton is famous for this dictum: "Power tends to corrupt and absolute power corrupts absolutely."

Nations need to be scattered and separated in order to maintain balance in the world. Nations need a system of checks and balances to prevent a concentration of economic, political, and military power.

God determined the exact times and places for nations to exist. The apostle Paul makes this point in his famous sermon on Mars Hill:

> From one man he [God] made all the nations, that they should inhabit the whole earth; and he marked out their appointed times in history and the boundaries of their lands.

God did this so that they would seek him and perhaps reach out for him and find him, though he is not far from any one of us.

Acts 17:26–27

Here we learn three great truths. First, God intends for us to inhabit the entire earth and not stay in one place. Second, God marks out the times for people groups and the places they should live, with land boundaries. Finally, God does these things so we will seek and find Him. God's ultimate purpose in everything He does is to reconcile mankind to Himself. When evil leaders try to gather power for a global government, God comes down to earth and scatters their efforts to the wind.

The Antichrist to Come

John the apostle wrote these sobering words: "The antichrist is coming." This person will emerge in the last days to conquer the world and establish a global government.

People often ask, Will he control the whole world? No, the Antichrist will fight resistance during the Great Tribulation but will meet his final end at Armageddon. The only global leadership we need is the return of Jesus Christ.

The return of Christ is the theme of both of Paul's letters to the church at Thessalonica, referring to it in every chapter. Paul's second letter to the Thessalonians paints a portrait of the coming Antichrist. He will seek to gain control of the world; he will be inspired by demonic power; and he will persecute God's people. Most importantly, the Antichrist will be destroyed when our Lord returns.

The Return of Christ

Paul wrote 2 Thessalonians to clarify misunderstandings about Christ's return:

> Concerning the coming of our Lord Jesus Christ and our being gathered to him, we ask you, brothers and sisters, not to become easily unsettled or alarmed by the teaching allegedly from us—whether by a prophecy or by word of mouth or by letter—asserting that the day of the Lord has already come.
>
> 2 Thessalonians 2:1–2

Misguided preachers and false prophets still try to get believers unsettled in their faith and alarmed by their speculations and so-called prophecies, which are little more than shallow sensationalism.

The Rise of the Antichrist

We learn about the sequence of events around Christ's return:

> Don't let anyone deceive you in any way, for that day [the coming of our Lord] will not come until the rebellion occurs and the man of lawlessness is revealed, the man doomed to destruction. He will oppose and will exalt himself over everything that is called God or is worshiped, so that he sets himself up in God's temple, proclaiming himself to be God.
>
> 2 Thessalonians 2:3–4

"The rebellion" is the Greek for *apostasy*, meaning a departure from the Christian faith. "The Spirit clearly says that in later times some will abandon the faith and follow deceiving spirits and things taught by demons" (1 Timothy 4:1). The current suppression of free speech by politicians, businesses, and media platforms is aimed partially at suppressing the truth of the Gospel and Scripture in an effort toward bowing to political correctness and secular views opposed to the Word of God. These leaders and groups advocate a false tolerance for everything except the truth.

In Paul's passage, then, we find an important personal challenge: "Don't let anyone deceive you in any way." Guard your heart and mind from deception by knowing what the Bible reveals about Jesus' return.

The Restraint of the Antichrist

God does not allow any evil politician or dictator to reach his or her goals. God's sovereignty limits evil activity in the world:

> Now you know what is holding him back, so that he may be revealed at the proper time. For the secret power of lawlessness is already at work; but the one who now holds it back will continue to do so till he is taken out of the way.
>
> 2 Thessalonians 2:6–7

The Spirit of God and the power of a Spirit-filled church proclaiming the Gospel holds back the rise of the Antichrist until God allows it.

The Revelation of the Antichrist

People are asking, Is the Antichrist alive in the world today? When will he appear? From what nation will he arise to power?

Then the lawless one will be revealed, whom the Lord Jesus will overthrow with the breath of his mouth and destroy by the splendor of his coming. The coming of the lawless one will be in accordance with how Satan works. He will use all sorts of displays of power through signs and wonders that serve the lie, and all the ways that wickedness deceives those who are perishing. They perish because *they refused to love the truth and so be saved.*

2 Thessalonians 2:8–10, emphasis added

God will hold the Antichrist back until the appointed time. Sadly the world will be deceived by his fake miracles and empty political promises. He will offer more and more ways for people to indulge themselves in all sorts of evil.

Here we read one of the saddest statements in the Bible about the resistance of humanity to God: "They perish because they refused to love the truth and so be saved." What is the truth? Or, more accurately, who is the truth? Jesus said, "I am the truth" (John 14:6). When you love Jesus, you love the truth. Jesus asked Peter after his denial, "Do you love me?" When people reject the truth of the Gospel and refuse the saving grace God offers them, they perish in this life and in the life to come.

We live in two dimensions, as Paul wrote: "Godliness has value for all things, holding promise for both the present life and the life to come" (1 Timothy 4:8). Don't spend all your time and money on this life; rather, invest in the life to come.

The Ruin of the Antichrist

The only government that is permanent is the Kingdom of God. The Antichrist—"whom the Lord Jesus will overthrow with the breath of his mouth and destroy by the splendor of his coming" (2 Thessalonians 2:8)—will meet his end when Jesus returns.

Where does the Antichrist end up? John the apostle saw his demise at Armageddon:

> Fire came down from heaven and devoured [the deceived nations]. And the devil, who deceived them, was thrown into the lake of burning sulfur, where the beast [i.e., the Antichrist] and the false prophet had been thrown.
>
> Revelation 20:9–10

Jesus said, "Then [the King] will say to those on his left, 'Depart from me, you who are cursed, into the eternal fire prepared for the devil and his angels'" (Matthew 25:41). Hell was not prepared for people but for the devil and his angels—the worst of which shall be the Antichrist.

Who else are the devil's angels? According to Paul the apostle, those who were leading the Corinthian church astray:

> Such people are false apostles, deceitful workers, masquerading as apostles of Christ. And no wonder, for Satan himself masquerades as an angel of light. It is not surprising, then, if his servants also masquerade as servants of righteousness. Their end will be what their actions deserve.
>
> 2 Corinthians 11:13–15

The Spirit of Antichrist

While we focus much attention on the person of the Antichrist, the spirit of antichrist is already at work in the world. As we read earlier:

Every spirit that acknowledges that Jesus Christ has come in the flesh is from God, but every spirit that does not acknowledge Jesus is not from God. *This is the spirit of the antichrist, which you have heard is coming and even now is already in the world.*

1 John 4:2–3, emphasis added

Faith begins with acknowledging Jesus as Savior. Jesus said, "Whoever acknowledges me before others, I will also acknowledge before my Father in heaven" (Matthew 10:32).

The word *acknowledge* means to come to know Jesus personally as your Lord and Savior. You see, the devil does not care if you study religion, go to religious services, participate in holy days, join a church, or take the sacraments. He just does not want you to acknowledge Jesus. The moment you acknowledge Jesus, you will be miraculously born again, be saved from sin and judgment, and have eternal life. "If you declare with your mouth, 'Jesus is Lord,' and believe in your heart that God raised him from the dead, you will be saved" (Romans 10:9).

British writer and scholar C. S. Lewis began his academic career at Oxford as an atheist. His anger toward God from childhood experiences led him to discount God's existence. As a boy of nine, he had watched his mother die from cancer. His prayers went unanswered, so he dismissed the existence of God, or at least the love of God. He considered the Bible little more than ancient folklore.

But while at Oxford, God started pulling at his heart. In his book *Surprised by Joy*, Lewis describes his struggle for faith. He likens God's pursuit to a fisherman and himself the fish, "and I never dreamed that the hook was in my tongue."

He describes his Christian conversion, meeting the One he had dreaded to meet:

> I gave in, and admitted that God was God, and knelt and prayed: perhaps, that night, the most dejected and reluctant convert in all England. I did not then see what is now the most shining and obvious thing: the Divine humility which will accept a convert even on such terms.[1]

If you are a prodigal, come home to God today by trusting Jesus Christ as your Savior and Lord. Today is the day of your salvation!

EIGHT

THE POWER BEHIND THE THRONE

C. S. Lewis in his classic book *The Screwtape Letters* writes: "There are two equal and opposite errors into which our race can fall about the devils. One is to disbelieve in their existence. The other is to believe, and to feel an excessive and unhealthy interest in them."[1]

I once heard that the devil does not want us to believe he exists, so he is always publishing the news of his death. The Bible speaks of "the mystery of iniquity" (2 Thessalonians 2:7 KJV). For centuries philosophers, preachers, and psychologists have studied the reality of evil—where it comes from, why it exists, and how it affects humanity. The Word of God is clear that there exists an alien power in this world, not an impersonal force but a personal being identified as Satan, who deceives humanity and opposes God.

An article in *The Atlantic* raises the question, Why are exorcisms on the rise? The story chronicles the strange demonic symptoms of people who were beyond psychological explanation or help.[2]

The percentage of people who believe in the devil as a type of evil is growing. According to YouGov research, more than half of Americans believe that demonic possession is real.[3]

Demons are mentioned eighty times in the Bible, along with six references to evil spirits and twenty-three references to unclean spirits. Jesus cast out demons and gave the same power to His disciples. Jesus taught us to pray, "Deliver us from evil." We are told, "Do not give the devil a foothold" (Ephesians 4:27). James wrote, "Resist the devil, and he will flee from you" (James 4:7). Paul wrote, "Our struggle is not against flesh and blood, but against . . . the spiritual forces of evil in the heavenly realms" (Ephesians 6:12). Spiritual forces of evil attack us, in part, through the world system. "We know that we are children of God, and that the whole world is under the control of the evil one" (1 John 5:19).

We have seen that the coming Antichrist is called "the man of lawlessness" (2 Thessalonians 2:3). He will be a world dictator operating under demonic power, control, and influence. History has seen its share of demonized dictators who have unleashed horrible suffering on humanity—Nero, the Roman emperor who persecuted the Church mercilessly; Adolf Hitler, who brought the Holocaust and the deaths of six million Jews; Joseph Stalin, the Russian czar who murdered millions of his own people in the name of Communism; and the Islamic jihadists who continue to inflict terrorism on the innocent. The list is endless. The coming Antichrist will be the worst of them all.

John the Revelator wrote: "The dragon stood on the shore of the sea. And I saw a beast coming out of the sea. . . . The

The Power behind the Throne

dragon gave the beast his power and his throne and great authority" (Revelation 13:1–2). The sea represents the restlessness of humanity and the political chaos and conflict of the last days. The Antichrist, the beast out of the sea, will derive his power from the dragon, Satan himself. The dragon is the power behind the throne, the architect of evil, who influences politicians and governments.

We live in a dual reality of the seen and the unseen, the natural and the spiritual. The untold evil done in our world by despots in government is the result of demonic influence over politicians.

Power, Throne, Authority

According to Revelation 13:2, the dragon will give the Antichrist three things: his power, his throne, and great authority.

Power

During Jesus' ministry there was a man possessed by demons who lived in a cemetery. He was so strong that the men of the town bound him with chains—but he broke the chains. He had great physical power because he was demon-possessed.

Jesus asked him, "What is your name?" The demons spoke through the man: "My name is Legion . . . for we are many" (Mark 5:9). When Jesus commanded the evil spirits to depart, the man was restored to complete health and became an evangelist for Christ.

The Antichrist's power and energy will be derived from Satanic influence. He will operate under demonic power. But John the apostle reassures us that the power of God in us is greater than the dark powers of this world (see 1 John

4:4). And Jesus promised, "You will receive power when the Holy Spirit comes on you" (Acts 1:8).

Throne

The devil will also give the Antichrist his throne—meaning his seat of political power. But the throne the devil gives is limited in scope and lasts only a short time. The devil always takes back what he gives, eventually leaving a person destitute.

The devil also offered to give Jesus a throne on which to rule:

> The devil took him to a very high mountain and showed him all the kingdoms of the world and their splendor. "All this will I give you," he said, "if you will bow down and worship me."
>
> Jesus said to him, "Away from me, Satan! For it is written: 'Worship the Lord your God, and serve him only.'"
>
> Then the devil left him.
>
> Matthew 4:8–11

Jesus refused the offer to worship, honor, and give place to the devil, and chose rather to bring us the Kingdom of God.

Great Authority

Not only will the Antichrist accept the devil's offer of a throne, but he will take his offer to rule the world.

The devil has made this offer to many politicians, dictators, and despots. The devil gives them power for a little while, then takes it away. Every evil kingdom and its potentate has perished over time, and their kingdoms have fallen. Jesus' Kingdom, however, is an eternal Kingdom. John the

The Power behind the Throne

Revelator heard the praise in heaven: "The kingdoms of this world have become the kingdoms of our Lord and of His Christ, and He shall reign forever and ever!" (Revelation 11:15 NKJV).

As believers we know "we are receiving a kingdom that cannot be shaken" (Hebrews 12:28).

When the Devil Runs for Office

While the last-days Antichrist is an actual world leader, a spirit of antichrist "even now is already in the world" (1 John 4:3). Spiritual forces of evil are at work in the world preparing the way for the coming Antichrist. Spiritual powers of evil are at work in politics.

The prophet Daniel discovered that the devil runs for office. While nations have kings, presidents, and prime ministers, there are often spiritual forces of evil that influence them and shape politics. Daniel was brought as a captive to Babylon after the invasion of Judah. He was promoted to political office under the reign of King Nebuchadnezzar. When Persia conquered Babylon, King Cyrus kept Daniel as a member of his administration because of Daniel's distinguished character and faithful service. In fact, Daniel was one of three governors who worked directly with the king and oversaw the entire kingdom of Persia, one of the largest kingdoms in history.

God gave Daniel prophetic visions of coming world empires. Daniel foretold in detail the coming of Persia and its defeat of Babylon; Greece under Alexander the Great; and the Roman Empire. He also foretold the coming of the Antichrist. Jesus quoted the prophecies of Daniel regarding His own return. The book of Revelation also uses the visions of Daniel to describe the last days.

135

Daniel prayed for the restoration of Israel, as God had promised through Jeremiah the prophet (see Daniel 9:2–4). He based his prayers on the promises of Scripture, just as we need to do.

While Daniel was in Persia, God gave him a revelation of "a great war" (Daniel 10:1). The word *great* means a true and burdensome war. He wanted to understand the revelation, and felt great sorrow and sadness in his heart as he considered the devastation of this coming war. He fasted and prayed for three weeks. Then he had another vision in which he saw a man whose face was like lightning, dressed in gleaming armor, whose his voice was "like the sound of a multitude" (verse 6). Others who were with him did not see the man, but were terrified because they could feel the presence of this great angel.

The angel's message to Daniel shows us the power behind the throne and how evil spirits influence governments. The angel said:

> "Do not be afraid, Daniel. Since the first day that you set your mind to gain understanding and to humble yourself before your God, your words were heard, and I have come in response to them. But *the prince of the Persian kingdom* resisted me twenty-one days. Then Michael, one of the chief princes, came to help me, because I was detained there with *the king of Persia*. Now I have come to explain to you what will happen to your people in the future, for the vision concerns a time yet to come."
>
> Daniel 10:12–14, emphasis added

Who is the prince of the Persian kingdom that resisted the angel of God? How is he different from the king of Persia,

The Power behind the Throne

who is also mentioned? The prince of Persia is obviously a spiritual being who ruled over that kingdom, while the king of Persia was a person. Michael the archangel had to assist this angel in the spiritual conflict with the prince of Persia. Then the angel told Daniel:

> "Do you know why I have come to you? Soon I will return to fight against the prince of Persia, and when I go, the prince of Greece will come. . . . No one supports me against them except Michael, your prince."
>
> Daniel 10:20–21

Historically we know that Greece defeated Persia. The fact that this angel fought against Persia means that God brought the kingdom of Persia to its end. Finally the angel referred to "Michael, your prince." The archangel Michael is the protector of God's people—Israel and the Church. Truly "the angel of the LORD encamps around those who fear him, and he delivers them" (Psalm 34:7).

John the apostle recorded a vision similar to that of Daniel: "Then war broke out in heaven. Michael and his angels fought against the dragon, and the dragon and his angels fought back. But he was not strong enough, and they lost their place in heaven" (Revelation 12:7–8). The dragon here is Satan, and his angels are evil spirits.

While I do not purport to understand all the implications of these passages, the truth speaks for itself. Evil forces influence politicians and governments, which helps explain the horrible oppression, tyranny, and destruction we see throughout history.

Wars on earth are often battles between good and evil in the heavenly realms. The spiritual and natural are inseparably connected.

Our struggle is not against flesh and blood, but against the rulers, against the authorities, against the powers of this dark world and against the spiritual forces of evil in the heavenly realms.

Ephesians 6:12

Notice how the apostle Paul used political titles—*rulers, authorities, powers*—to refer to evil spirits at work in our world. In the same passage Paul referred to "the day of evil" (verse 13), meaning the influence of evil on natural and historical events. The only weapon against evil is the spiritual authority, grace, and power Jesus has given us to live as more than conquerors.

Murder and Lies

The devil is a deceiver. Jesus told the corrupt leaders of His day:

> "You belong to your father, the devil, and you want to carry out your father's desires. He was a murderer from the beginning, not holding to the truth, for there is no truth in him. When he lies, he speak his native language, for he is a liar and the father of lies."

John 8:44

Jesus revealed how the devil works in political structures and ecclesiastical organizations. He influences men whose hearts are evil to do what he desires—namely, to war against God by deceiving and destroying humanity.

The devil has two diabolical characteristics. First, he is "a murderer from the beginning"—referring to the first murder, when Cain, taken over by rage and jealousy, killed his

The Power behind the Throne

innocent and righteous brother, Abel. The devil lurks behind the merciless bloodshed of the righteous throughout history. Horrible acts of evil have been perpetuated by people in positions of power, people who are subhuman because of demonic possession.

Second, Jesus called the devil "a liar and the father of lies." Satan deceives people, as he deceived Eve in the Garden, in order to destroy humanity. "The god of this age has blinded the minds of unbelievers, so that they cannot see the light of the gospel that displays the glory of Christ, who is the image of God" (2 Corinthians 4:4). We cannot understand the world in which we live, the atrocities of history, and the untold evil coming with the rise of the Antichrist on the world scene, if we don't understand the power behind the throne: "The dragon gave [the beast] his power" (Revelation 13:2).

John the Revelator gave us a graphic description of the dragon. After war broke out in heaven, and Michael and his angels defeated the dragon and his angels, "the great dragon was hurled down—that ancient serpent called the devil, or Satan, who leads the whole world astray. He was hurled to the earth, and his angels with him" (Revelation 12:9). One phrase in that passage describes the devil's motive and method: He "leads the whole world astray."

Evil forces are at work in the world to lead humanity away from God, away from Jesus as Savior, and away from God's purpose for our lives. Evil forces also work inside the Church to bring deception to weaken the Church and her witness and work.

Look at how Jesus described Satan's work in the Church. When the Gospel is preached and the Church is established, the devil shows up to undermine the work of God:

> "Listen then to what the parable of the sower means: When anyone hears the message about the kingdom and does not understand it, the evil one comes and snatches away what was sown in their heart. This is the seed sown along the path."
>
> Matthew 13:18–19

Someone hears the Gospel of God and does not fully understand it or believe it, and the evil one—that is, Satan—steals the Word of God from that person's heart. That is why some people have to hear the Gospel several times before the root of faith starts to grow. We need to pray for our families, friends, and the world that the Holy Spirit will reveal Jesus Christ to them, just as He brings sight to the blind.

Jesus also explained in the parable of the weeds how Satan works to undermine the work of God:

> "The kingdom of heaven is like a man who sowed good seed in his field. But while everyone was sleeping, his enemy came and sowed weeds among the wheat, and went away. When the wheat sprouted and formed heads, then the weeds also appeared."
>
> Matthew 13:24–26

The devil sows the weeds (false doctrine) among the wheat (the Word of God).

Paul the apostle prophesied:

> The Spirit clearly says that in later times some will abandon the faith and follow deceiving spirits and things taught by demons. Such teachings come through hypocritical liars, whose consciences have been seared as with a hot iron.
>
> 1 Timothy 4:1–2

Look carefully at this passage. People will "follow deceiving spirits and things taught by demons"—and it comes through misguided people, "hypocritical liars." These false teachers, "whose consciences have been seared," are deceived, so they naturally deceive the people who follow them.

Paul cautions us that false teachers are "masquerading as apostles of Christ. And no wonder, for Satan himself masquerades as an angel of light" (2 Corinthians 11:13–14). In the name *Antichrist* is the name *Christ*. This person will come as a *false* Messiah who imitates the message and ministry of Jesus.

Remember Jesus' instruction:

> "Watch out that no one deceives you. For many will come in my name, claiming, 'I am the Messiah,' and will deceive many. . . . For *false messiahs and false prophets* will appear and perform great signs and wonders to deceive, if possible, even the elect. See, I have told you ahead of time."
>
> Matthew 24:4–5, 24–25, emphasis added

There is simply no way to understand world history to date and the coming world order under the Antichrist without understanding the demonic realm. Again, mark carefully these words: "The dragon gave the beast his power" (Revelation 13:2). Satan himself is the power behind the throne.

I know we live in the most advanced time in history with science and technology. Yet who can dismiss the existence of evil? We live in a modern world, yet we continue to witness untold evil, with violence, hatred, and oppression, because human beings are led astray by the evil one to do his bidding rather than the will of God.

Why did Judas Iscariot, one of the Twelve, betray Jesus? He lived with Jesus for three years, trained and commissioned as an apostle. Yet at the end, his greed and selfishness opened the door of his heart to the demonic. Before the Last Supper, we read these startling words:

Then Satan entered Judas, called Iscariot, one of the Twelve. And Judas went to the chief priests and the officers of the temple guard and discussed with them how he might betray Jesus. They were delighted and agreed to give him money. He consented, and watched for an opportunity to hand Jesus over to them when no crowd was present.

Luke 22:3–6, emphasis added

Jesus referred to Judas as "the son of perdition" (John 17:12 NKJV). Later Paul ascribed the same title to the Antichrist (see 2 Thessalonians 2:3). *Son of perdition* means *son of destruction*, or the one doomed to destruction. Judas and the Antichrist are the only two men in the Bible called "the son of perdition," because they were both to do the devil's bidding.

At the end Judas threw away the thirty pieces of silver and hanged himself. When the devil gives a person power and position, he will eventually take it back and leave the person desolate. Jesus, on the other hand, gives us life and life more abundantly.

At the end of time, the beast (the Antichrist) will be thrown into the lake of fire:

Fire came down from heaven and devoured [the deceived nations]. And the devil, who deceived them, was thrown into the lake of burning sulfur, where the beast [i.e., the Antichrist] and the false prophet had been thrown.

Revelation 20:9–10

Door to the Demonic

On Valentine's Day 2018, a disturbed teenager named Nikolas Cruz shot and killed seventeen students and staff members at a high school in Parkland, Florida, and injured seventeen others in a mass shooting. He confessed to the crime and claimed that he heard demon voices in his head telling him to carry out the deadly attack.[4]

I have never seen the devil or demons, but I have seen their effects. I have never seen the wind, but I have felt its effects. I have never seen electricity, but I have seen its effects. I have never seen microwaves and radio waves, but I have seen their effects. The same logic must be applied to spiritual forces of evil at work in the spiritual realm.

When Jesus' seventy-two disciples returned from preaching in towns and villages, saying joyfully, "Lord, even the demons submit to us in your name," Jesus replied:

> "I saw Satan fall like lightning from heaven. I have given you authority to trample on snakes and scorpions and to overcome all the power of the enemy; nothing will harm you. However, do not rejoice that the spirits submit to you, but rejoice that your names are written in heaven."

Luke 10:17–20

Here Jesus validated the reality of Lucifer's expulsion from heaven and the existence of demons, fallen angels seeking to destroy us, the object of God's redeeming love. Jesus gave His disciples authority over demons ("snakes and scorpions") and the assurance of divine protection ("Nothing will harm you").

The human struggle, as we know, is against spiritual forces of evil and not merely natural forces (which also bring suffering). Paul the apostle opened the door of understanding to the demonic, so we can see how they operate:

> We do not wrestle against flesh and blood, but against principalities, against powers, against the rulers of the darkness of this age, against spiritual hosts of wickedness in the heavenly places. Therefore take up the whole armor of God, that you may be able to withstand in the evil day, and having done all, to stand.
>
> Ephesians 6:12–13 NKJV

The work of demons is clearly seen in the last days when judgment comes to the world:

> I saw a star [angel] fallen from heaven to the earth. To him was given the key to the bottomless pit. And he opened the bottomless pit, and smoke arose out of the pit like the smoke of a great furnace. . . . Then out of the smoke locusts came upon the earth. And to them was given power, as the scorpions of the earth have power. . . .
>
> Their power was to hurt men five months. And they had as king over them the angel of the bottomless pit, whose name in Hebrew is Abaddon, but in Greek he has the name Apollyon.
>
> Revelation 9:1–3, 10–11 NKJV

You may say about these locusts, "That's just symbolism." It is—but I ask you what reality the symbol describes.

The Power behind the Throne

A symbol represents something real. The graphic language in this passage gives us understanding of the suffering and torment that demonic powers will bring on humanity. The good news is that these demon locusts will afflict only evil people:

> They were told not to harm the grass of the earth or any plant or tree, but *only those people who did not have the seal of God on their foreheads.* They were not allowed to kill them but only to torture them for five months. . . . During those days people will seek death but will not find it; they will long to die, but death will elude them.
>
> verses 4–6, emphasis added

The people afflicted in this way will be followers of the Antichrist and bear his seal, the mark of the Beast, 666, and not "the seal of God." Also note the reference to scorpions, which Jesus said describes demons and their work of affliction. God's people, however, have been "sealed for the day of redemption" (Ephesians 4:30).

In the following passage, demons—like frogs!—will draw world leaders and their armies to Armageddon. (In the next chapter, we will discuss their final end.)

> The sixth angel poured out his bowl on the great river Euphrates, and its water was dried up to prepare the way for the kings from the East. Then I saw *three impure spirits* that looked like frogs; they came out of the mouth of the dragon, out of the mouth of the beast and out of the mouth of the false prophet. *They are demonic spirits* that perform signs, and they go out to the kings of the whole world, to gather them for the battle on the great day of God Almighty.

145

"Look, I come like a thief! Blessed is the one who stays awake and remains clothed, so as not to go naked and be shamefully exposed."

Then they gathered the kings together to the place that in Hebrew is called Armageddon.

Revelation 16:12–16, emphasis added

Look at the wording very carefully—three *impure spirits* came out of the mouth of the dragon (the devil), and *demonic spirits* performed signs and gathered the kings to Armageddon. What a portrait of how demons influence world events by deceiving corrupt politicians and luring them to their final end at Armageddon.

Total Victory

Just as Jesus gave His disciples power and authority over demons, He has given us the same power and authority. Jesus' disciples rejoiced that "even the demons submit to us in your name." The name of Jesus, when invoked by faith, overcomes demonic power. Recall Jesus' emphatic response: "I saw Satan fall like lightning from heaven."

In his *Navigation Plan 2021*, Admiral Michael Gilday of the U.S. Navy wrote: "Our Sailors must be able to outthink and outfight any adversary."[5] In the same way, believers must understand our enemy if we expect to outthink and outfight them. The apostle Paul urged "that Satan might not outwit us. For we are not unaware of his schemes" (2 Corinthians 2:11). The word *schemes* mean strategies, tactics, plans, purposes, and cunning. But victory is ours over demonic intrusion and influence. When the devil is portrayed in Revelation persecuting the Church, the Church overcomes his assault:

The Power behind the Throne

The accuser of our brothers and sisters, who accuses them before our God day and night, has been hurled down. They triumphed over him by the blood of the Lamb and by the word of their testimony; they did not love their lives so much as to shrink from death. Therefore rejoice, you heavens and you who dwell in them! But woe to the earth and the sea, because the devil has gone down to you! He is filled with fury, because he knows that his time is short.

Revelation 12:10–12

Satan is a defeated enemy living on borrowed time, because the powers of darkness were defeated at Calvary: "Having disarmed the powers and authorities, he [Jesus] made a public spectacle of them, triumphing over them by the cross" (Colossians 2:15).

The House of Rothchild, a historical film from 1934, dramatically portrayed of the defeat of Napoleon at the Battle of Waterloo by the Duke of Wellington and two armies of the Seventh Coalition. In the movie and historically, although Nathan Rothschild had risked his wealth to support the allies, Napoleon appeared invincible, so the English breathlessly awaited word of the battle's outcome. At first the message relayed by Morse code across the foggy English Channel seemed to bring dire news: "Wellington defeated." Suddenly the fog cleared and the rest of the message came through: "Wellington defeated the enemy!"[6]

Calvary was Satan's Waterloo. It is the place where sin, death, and judgment were defeated and humanity was redeemed. When Jesus died on the cross, the disciples felt their Lord had been defeated. Then Sunday morning came, and Jesus arose from the dead in victory.

At Calvary the grace of God gives us true spiritual wealth in this life plus "treasures in heaven" (Matthew 6:20). Paul wrote that, in Jesus, "we have redemption through his blood, the forgiveness of sins, in accordance with the riches of God's grace that he lavished on us" (Ephesians 1:7–8). We are both redeemed and rich in Christ, living on "the boundless riches of Christ" (Ephesians 3:8).

The name *Satan* means "adversary," and the title *devil* means "accuser." The devil is defeated by the victory of Jesus' death and resurrection, but he is not destroyed until the end of time. Right now, "Your enemy the devil prowls around like a roaring lion looking for someone to devour. Resist him, standing firm in the faith" (1 Peter 5:8–9). When we stand firm in the faith, we can resist the powers of evil at work in the world. The Holy Spirit and the Spirit-filled Church, as we have seen, are the restraining force in the world against evil.

A book by Paul E. Billheimer, *Destined for the Throne*, has made a lasting impression on me. He makes the challenge that "any church without a well-organized and systematic prayer program is simply treading a religious treadmill." Bilheimer's insights on prayer are thought-provoking:

> Prayer is not begging God to do something which He is loath to do. It is not overcoming reluctance in God. It is enforcing Christ's victory over Satan. It is implementing upon earth Heaven's decisions concerning the affairs of men. Calvary legally destroyed Satan, and canceled all of his claims. God placed the enforcement of Calvary's victory in the hand of the Church. He has given her "power of attorney." She is His "deputy." But this delegated authority is wholly inoperative apart from the prayers of a believing Church. Therefore, prayer is where the action is.[7]

Counterfeit Faith

People are misled and deceived because Satan's counterfeit looks so much like the truth. As we have seen, he masquerades as an angel of light.

When I was a teenager, I heard a pastor explain how spiritual counterfeits mimic the Gospel of Christ. When banking and law enforcement officials are trained in detecting counterfeit currency, he said, they don't study the details of counterfeit bills. Instead, they study every intricate detail and nuance of genuine currency. Once they are intimately acquainted with the real, they can easily detect the counterfeit.

Paul the apostle cautioned the Corinthian believers not to "be led astray from your sincere and pure devotion to Christ" (2 Corinthians 11:3). The word *sincere* means "genuine." We follow Jesus with single-mindedness, looking away from distractions and false doctrine. Paul continued:

> If someone comes to you and preaches a Jesus other than the Jesus we preached, or if you receive a different spirit from the Spirit you received, or a different gospel from the one you accepted, you put up with it easily enough.
>
> 2 Corinthians 11:4

Unlike the church at Corinth, we need to be good judges of character so no one leads us astray.

The story goes that a feisty little dog was always getting into fights with other dogs and losing. Once, while watching his dog get into a fight and suffer the usual beating, a friend said to the man, "That dog of yours isn't much of a fighter, is he?"

The man responded, "On the contrary, he's an excellent fighter. He's just a bad judge of dogs. He always underestimates his adversaries."

The Galatian church was challenged for being too gullible and unguarded in her faith:

> I am astonished that you are so quickly deserting the one who called you to live in the grace of Christ and are turning to a different gospel—which is really no gospel at all. Evidently some people are throwing you into confusion and are trying to pervert the gospel of Christ. But even if we or an angel from heaven should preach a gospel other than the one we preached to you, let them be under God's curse!
>
> Galatians 1:6–8

Strong words but true.

William of Ockham, a fourteenth-century theologian, gave us what is called "Occam's razor," the principle of parsimony. This problem-solving principle recommends looking for explanations constructed with the fewest possible set of elements. The principle can be paraphrased as "The simplest explanation is usually the best one."

The Gospel of Jesus and the Bible are simple enough for a child to understand. In fact, Jesus said, "Unless you change and become like little children, you will never enter the kingdom of heaven" (Matthew 18:3). The Christian faith is simple. Jesus said, "Take my yoke upon you and learn from me. . . . For my yoke is easy and my burden is light" (Matthew 11:29–30).

When people search after sensational signs, they may get misled. We are urged not to "be carried away by all kinds of strange teachings" (Hebrews 13:9). So if a minister, message,

The Power behind the Throne

or ministry seems strange and weird to you, there is a high probability that it *is* weird. Your intuition is usually correct. The Holy Spirit is giving you discernment to protect you.

When we consider the coming deception in the last days, we are challenged by the apostle Peter:

> Therefore, dear friends, since you have been forewarned, be on your guard so that you may not be carried away by the error of the lawless and fall from your secure position. But grow in the grace and knowledge of our Lord and Savior Jesus Christ.
>
> 2 Peter 3:17–18

As the Day of Christ draws closer, let us guard our hearts and our doctrine as we grow strong in the grace and knowledge of the Lord Jesus. Guard and grow! By doing so, you will keep yourself and your family spiritually safe and secure against all harm.

NINE

THE WAR TO END ALL WARS

The motto of the Apollo 11 mission on July 20, 1969, was, "We came in peace for all mankind."[1] This motto appears on the plaque left on the surface of the moon, where the astronauts landed on the Sea of Tranquility. Astronauts Neil Armstrong and Buzz Aldrin found themselves in a wonderfully peaceful place on the moon. Why? Because there were no people living there.

When sin entered the world through Adam and Eve, peace was forfeited. Ever since Cain murdered his brother, Abel, humanity has sought desperately for world peace. It has been observed that in the last four thousand years of human history, there have not been one hundred consecutive years of peace.

Perhaps nothing is more tragic than war. The psalmist David said, "I am for peace; but when I speak, they are for war" (Psalm 120:7). The Bible reveals that the future is destined for war: "The end will come like a flood: War will

153

continue until the end, and desolations have been decreed" (Daniel 9:26). Jesus said there will be "wars and rumors of wars. . . . Nation will rise against nation, and kingdom against kingdom" (Matthew 24:6–7).

World leaders try to negotiate peace, but most peace treaties fail over time. World peace is fragile. Paul the apostle writes,

> Now, brothers and sisters, about times and dates we do not need to write to you, for you know very well that the day of the Lord will come like a thief in the night. While people are saying, "Peace and safety," destruction will come on them suddenly, as labor pains on a pregnant woman, and they will not escape.
>
> 1 Thessalonian 5:1–3

True peace will come to this world only when Jesus Christ, the Prince of Peace, returns.

World War I was called the war to end all wars. It was not—but the final war is coming at the battle of Armageddon, when the Antichrist and a coalition of nations will attack Israel and her allies. Suddenly the skies will part, and Jesus will return to defeat the Antichrist kingdom and reign as King of kings.

Let's listen to Jesus talk about His return at the end of the Tribulation:

> "Immediately after the tribulation of those days . . . the sign of the Son of Man will appear in heaven, and then all the tribes of the earth will mourn, and they will see the Son of Man coming on the clouds of heaven with power and great glory."
>
> Matthew 24:29–30 NKJV

War Games

The name *Armageddon* is from the Hebrew *Har Megiddo*, meaning the hill or mountain of Megiddo. The word appears only in Revelation 16:16 and refers to a valley in northern Israel. The Bible also refers to it as the Valley of Jezreel, where several battles were fought; "the Valley of Jehoshaphat" (Joel 3:2), meaning "the Lord judges"; and "the valley of decision" (Joel 3:14). Napoleon referred to it as the most natural battlefield in the world. This final battle will take place "on the great day of God Almighty" (Revelation 16:14).

Megiddo was a Canaanite stronghold in the Jezreel plain in northern Israel, which was captured by the Israelites during the campaigns of Joshua (see Joshua 12:21; Judges 5:19). The valley begins at Megiddo and stretches some 180 miles south to the Gulf of Aqaba. This valley has been the site of many historic battles. It was here that Barak and Deborah conquered Sisera (see Judges 5:19–20); where King Ahaziah died by the arrows of Jehu (see 2 Kings 9:27); and where the godly king Josiah died in battle with Pharaoh Necho (see 2 Kings 23:29–30). Megiddo was the location of the famous stables of Solomon that held 450 chariot horses, a place that can be toured today.

Armageddon refers to a spiritual war between good and evil. It is caused by "demonic spirits that . . . go out to the kings of the whole world, to gather them for the battle on the great day of God Almighty" (Revelation 16:14). Look at that phrase *demonic spirits*. These spirits, as we saw in the last chapter, will draw kings and nations to their final end at Armageddon. Demonic spirits drive nations to war. This means that Armageddon is a spiritual war as well as a natural war, where Jesus will defeat the forces of evil for all time.

At Armageddon, Jesus will return with power and glory to destroy the Antichrist kingdom and establish the eternal Kingdom of God. The end of the age as we know it is the beginning of a new world order under the righteous rule of Jesus Christ.

Prophetic Preview

An overview of Bible prophecy about the battle of Armageddon puts the magnitude of this final conflict into perspective.

The Vision of Ezekiel

Ezekiel was a priest and prophet who grew up in Babylon during the days of the Babylonian captivity. He described a war in which God brings a ruler referred to as *Gog* (the Antichrist) and *Magog* (the land of Gog) into conflict at Armageddon. These titles *Gog* and *Magog* represent nations in rebellion against God. It will take seven months to bury the corpses of the soldiers slain in the conflict at "the great supper of God" (Revelation 19:17).

God revealed Armageddon to Ezekiel:

"Son of man, prophesy against Gog [the Antichrist] and say: 'This is what the Sovereign LORD says: I am against you, Gog, chief prince of Meshek and Tubal. I will turn you around and drag you along. I will bring you from the far north and send you against the mountains of Israel. Then I will strike your bow from your left hand and make your arrows drop from your right hand. On the mountains of Israel you will fall, you and all your troops and the nations with you. . . . And they will know that I am the LORD.

"'On that day I will give Gog a burial place in Israel, in the valley of those who travel east of the Sea. . . . So it will be called the Valley of Hamon Gog.

"'For seven months the Israelites will be burying them [Gog and all his hordes] in order to cleanse the land.'"

Ezekiel 39:1–6, 11–12

The Vision of Zechariah

One of the dramatic visions of Armageddon and the Millennium is given by the prophet Zechariah:

> A day of the LORD is coming, Jerusalem, when your possessions will be plundered and divided up within your very walls. I will gather all the nations to Jerusalem to fight against it; the city will be captured. . . . Then the LORD will go out and fight against those nations, as he fights on a day of battle. On that day his feet will stand on the Mount of Olives, east of Jerusalem, and the Mount of Olives will be split in two. . . . Then the LORD my God will come, and all the holy ones with him.

Zechariah 14:1–5

Zechariah may describe nuclear war:

> This is the plague with which the LORD will strike all the nations that fought against Jerusalem: Their flesh will rot while they are still standing on their feet, their eyes will rot in their sockets, and their tongues will rot in their mouths.

Zechariah 14:12

The Vision of Joel

The prophet Joel saw multitudes drawn into this war in the valley of decision:

"In those days and at that time, when I restore the fortunes of Judah and Jerusalem, I will gather all nations and bring them down to the Valley of Jehoshaphat. There I will put them on trial for what they did to my inheritance, my people Israel, because they scattered my people among the nations and divided up my land."

Joel 3:1–2

Joel continued the prophecy:

Proclaim this among the nations: Prepare for war! Rouse the warriors! Let all the fighting men draw near and attack. Beat your plowshares into swords and your pruning hooks into spears. . . . Bring down your warriors, LORD!

"Let the nations be roused; let them advance into the Valley of Jehoshaphat, for there I will sit to judge all the nations on every side."

verses 9–12

He described the war in graphic detail:

Multitudes, multitudes in the valley of decision! For the day of the LORD is near in the valley of decision. The sun and moon will be darkened, and the stars no longer shine. The LORD will roar from Zion and thunder from Jerusalem; the earth and the heavens will tremble. But the LORD will be a refuge for his people, a stronghold for the people of Israel.

"Then you will know that I, the LORD your God, dwell in Zion, my holy hill. Jerusalem will be holy; never again will foreigners invade her."

verses 14–17

The War to End All Wars

Finally God promises a new beginning after Armageddon:

"In that day the mountains will drip new wine, and the hills will flow with milk; all the ravines of Judah will run with water. A fountain will flow out of the LORD's house and will water the valley of acacias." . . .
The LORD dwells in Zion!

Joel 3:18, 21

The Prophecy of Jesus

Jesus described the final war of Armageddon and the glory of His return:

"As lightning that comes from the east is visible even in the west, so will be the coming of the Son of Man. . . . Immediately after the distress of those days 'the sun will be darkened, and the moon will not give its light; the stars will fall from the sky, and the heavenly bodies will be shaken.' Then will appear the sign of the Son of Man in heaven. And then all the peoples of the earth will mourn when they see the Son of Man coming on the clouds of heaven, with power and great glory."

Matthew 24:27, 29–30

The Prophecy of Paul

Paul told the Thessalonian church what will happen amid the splendor of the coming of Christ:

God is just: He will pay back trouble to those who trouble you and give relief to you who are troubled, and to us as well. This will happen when the Lord Jesus is revealed from heaven in blazing fire with his powerful angels. He will punish those who do not know God and do not obey the gospel of our Lord Jesus. They will be punished with everlasting destruction and shut out from the presence of the Lord and from the glory of his might on the day he comes to be glorified in his holy people and to be marveled at among all those who have believed.

2 Thessalonians 1:6–10

Paul reassured the Corinthians that, after Jesus returns and the dead are resurrected,

Then the end will come, when he hands over the kingdom to God the Father after he has destroyed all dominion, authority and power. For he must reign until he has put all his enemies under his feet. The last enemy to be destroyed is death.

1 Corinthians 15:24–26

The Visions of John

John the Revelator described the pouring out of the sixth bowl of wrath:

The sixth angel poured out his bowl on the great river Euphrates, and its water was dried up to prepare the way for the kings from the East.

Revelation 16:12

What is the significance of the Euphrates River? The Euphrates is the location of the cradle of civilization dating back to early Mesopotamia. Later ancient Babylon was built along the Euphrates River. Here, when the Euphrates dries up, it will allow "the kings from the East"

160

The War to End All Wars

to march across it toward Armageddon, where God will war against them.

John continued:

> Then I saw three impure spirits that looked like frogs; they came out of the mouth of the dragon, out of the mouth of the beast and out of the mouth of the false prophet. They are demonic spirits that perform signs, and they go out to the kings of the whole world, to gather them for the battle on the great day of God Almighty.
>
> verses 13–14

The kings of the East will be lured into battle by the influence of these demonic spirits "that looked like frogs." The fact that these spirits come out of the mouth of the dragon (Satan), the Beast (the Antichrist), and the false prophet depict that these kings will operate under the influence and propaganda of the Antichrist.

Frogs were considered unclean by the Jews (see Leviticus 11:41). This probably dates to the plague of frogs brought on the Egyptians, who viewed the frog as a symbol of the goddess Heqt, a frog-headed goddess of birth and fertility. The Persians thought of the frog as a double of Ahriman, god of evil and agent of plagues.[2]

The book of Revelation describes the battle of Armageddon:

> The angel swung his sickle on the earth, gathered its grapes and threw them into the great winepress of God's wrath. They were trampled in the winepress outside the city, and blood flowed out of the press, rising as high as the horses' bridles for a distance of 1,600 stadia.
>
> Revelation 14:19–20

John the Revelator also said that the battle will take place "outside the city," referring to the city of Jerusalem. It will be so great that the blood will flow as high as the horses' bridles for 180 miles.

When the sixth trumpet sounds, the angel is told:

> "Release the four angels who are bound at the great river Euphrates." And the four angels who had been kept ready for this very hour and day and month and year were released to kill a third of mankind. The number of the mounted troops was twice ten thousand times ten thousand. I heard their number.
>
> Revelation 9:14–16

During the first century, when the book of Revelation was written, it was inconceivable that an army from the East would number two hundred million; but today, with China's population and army, we can indeed envision such a massive army assembled at Armageddon.

The Second Coming

Armageddon represents more than a war fought over lands, wealth, and resources. It is the final spiritual conflict, as we have seen, between good and evil. Jesus Christ will return in triumphant glory at Armageddon to destroy the Antichrist and his kingdom and to establish the eternal Kingdom of God.

The New Testament uses three Greek words to describe the advent of Christ at Armageddon. First, Jesus' return is a *parousia*, which means a personal appearing. It was used to describe the appearance of a king in his royal procession when he paid a personal visit to a province in his kingdom.

The Second Coming is not metaphorical language. Jesus will return literally, visibly, and victoriously to reign as Lord over politics, economics, ecology, society, and more.

His coming is called an *epiphany* to signify a sudden and dramatic appearing. His entry into the world in Bethlehem was quiet, peaceful, and unnoticed. His return at the end of the age will come with a flash of lightning from the east to the west, as we have seen, and with the voice of the archangel and the trumpet of God. He will come with the clouds of heaven and with a host of angels, and "every eye will see him" (Revelation 1:7).

Finally, Jesus' return is called an *apocalypse*, meaning an unveiling. It is the Greek word for *revelation*—literally, the apocalypse. When Jesus returns, His divinity will not be veiled by the garment of humanity. Rather, the world will see Him in all His heavenly glory. His face will be like the sun shining in all its strength. He will not return as the baby in Bethlehem, the teacher of parables, the preacher of the Gospel, or the miracle worker. Rather, He will come bearing the name that is above every name.

John the Revelator describes Jesus' victorious return at Armageddon:

> I saw heaven standing open and there before me was a white horse, whose rider is called Faithful and True. With justice he judges and wages war. . . . The armies of heaven were following him. . . . Coming out of his mouth is a sharp sword with which to strike down the nations. "He will rule them with an iron scepter." He treads the winepress of the fury of the wrath of God Almighty. On his robe and on his thigh, he has this name written: KING OF KINGS AND LORD OF LORDS.

> Revelation 19:11, 14–16

When Jesus returns, the Antichrist kingdom will be destroyed:

> Then I saw the beast [the Antichrist] and the kings of the earth and their armies gathered together to wage war against the rider on the horse and his army. But the beast was captured, and with it the false prophet who had performed the signs on its behalf. With these signs he had deluded those who had received the mark of the beast and worshiped its image. The two of them were thrown alive into the fiery lake of burning sulfur. The rest were killed with the sword coming out of the mouth of the rider on the horse, and all the birds gorged themselves on their flesh.

Revelation 19:19–21

Armageddon is not a tragic end to human history. Rather, it is the prelude to a new world order, as Jesus "will reign on David's throne and over his kingdom, establishing and upholding it with justice and righteousness from that time on and forever. The zeal of the LORD Almighty will accomplish this" (Isaiah 9:7).

The return of Jesus Christ will usher us into God's fantastic future of the new heavens and the new earth. Keep reading and learn what God has in store for us.

I want to share a poem I wrote concerning the Lord's return and what it means for us to be ready when He comes.

WHERE WILL YOU BE?
Where will you be when the moon turns to blood,
when desolation and wars consume like a flood?
Where will you be when the stars fall to the earth,
when God gives the world a glorious new birth?
Where will you be?

The War to End All Wars

Where will you be when the last trumpet sounds,
when the great earthquake trembles the ground?
Where will you be when the signs are fulfilled,
when the suffering of humanity will finally be
    healed?
Where will you be?

Look! He is coming in the clouds of glory;
He's coming with a flaming sword in His hand.
Look! He is coming in truth and justice.
Christ is coming—but who can stand?

Where will you be when the seven seals are broken,
when the trumpet sounds the final hour?
Where will you be when the armies march together,
when they stand on Armageddon's brow?
Where will you be?

Will you be found true and faithful?
Will you wear the victor's crown?
Will your works pass the final judgment?
Will your soul in Christ be found?
Where will you be?

Look! He is coming in the clouds of glory;
He's coming with a flaming sword in His hand.
Look! He is coming in truth and justice.
Take your stand—and having done all, may you stand.

TEN

GLOBAL WARMING

People worry about the weather. Young people, when asked what concerns them, rank climate high on their list of worries. The concept of weather, according to NASA, refers to changes in atmospheric conditions—such as rain, snow, wind, or thunderstorms—locally over a short period. Climate refers to temperature, humidity, and rainfall over longer periods, at least thirty years. Global warming is the heating up of the surface of the earth over a long time—dating back to the Industrial Revolution—due to human activity.[1]

A few months before this writing, the United States experienced an intense heat wave, with one-third of Americans on a heat alert. Many other heat waves have been similar. According to some data I have compiled: A European drought in 1540 lasted eleven months. A North American heat wave in July 1757 was the hottest on record until 2003. A heat wave during the Dust Bowl and the Depression in

1936 caused the destruction of crops and five thousand deaths, and it followed the coldest winter on record.

The Bible tells us that when Christ returns, the earth will be renovated and restored by fire to be a new earth:

> The day of the Lord will come like a thief. The heavens will disappear with a roar; the elements will be destroyed by fire, and the earth and everything done in it will be laid bare. . . . That day will bring about the destruction of the heavens by fire, and the elements will melt in the heat. But in keeping with his promise we are looking forward to a new heaven and a new earth, where righteousness dwells.
>
> 2 Peter 3:10, 12–13

Take note of the key words *heavens*, *elements*, *fire*, *earth*, *melt*, and *heat*. The fire and heat could refer to environmental conditions or to a regional nuclear war. These terms could also mean spiritual refinement. While fire can destroy, it also purifies and refines. Destruction by fire is not the obliteration of the earth but the destruction of the current age of sin and suffering. God will re-create and restore the world to its original state of perfection.

Fire is a biblical symbol of God's purifying word. Jesus baptizes us with fire (see Matthew 3:11). He said, "I have come to bring fire on the earth" (Luke 12:49). When the Holy Spirit came at Pentecost, the believers "saw what seemed to be tongues of fire that separated and came to rest on each of them" (Acts 2:3). We are instructed, "Do not put out the Spirit's fire" (1 Thessalonians 5:19 NIV1984).

The destruction of the earth by fire, then, could be physical or spiritual in nature. God destroys the old order of sin and suffering and creates a new world. The good news is that

Global Warming

He will use fire to bring about the renovation or renewal of the earth. And when Christ returns, He will bring about a true new world order.

Renovation Work

Home renovation is big business. Most homeowners will do a major renovation on their homes at some point. Renovating a house is usually cheaper than buying a new one. When we renovate, we make our current house new. But renovation work is messy. It begins with the demolition and destruction of the old before we start developing the new.

God will do the same thing to the earth when Jesus returns.

This terrestrial ball on which we live is almost 25,000 miles in circumference and nearly 8,000 miles in diameter. Scientists tells us that the earth was formed about 4.5 billion years ago. The core of the earth is filled with molten elements, primarily iron and nickel, and is thousands of degrees Fahrenheit.

Maybe the unleashing of these boiling elements will cause the earth to become a ball of fire as God's renovation work takes place. As the apostle Peter said, the day of Jesus' return "will bring about the destruction of the heavens by fire, and the elements will melt in the heat" (2 Peter 3:12).

Fire is used in the Bible to describe God's work of purification. Fire both destroys and renews. Some scholars view the reference to fire as being a regional nuclear war at Armageddon. No one knows for sure how the renovation by fire will happen. The fire could be a literal fire or a spiritual flame. One thing is for certain—God will purify this world and make a new home for us.

The earth will not be totally destroyed by the fire, but purified and renovated into a better world—the home of righteousness, as Peter said. God's fire will cleanse everything that is not right in His eyes and create a world in which righteousness and peace form the climate of life. In His time, God will give us a new world. The end of this age will be the beginning of a new age with a new heaven and a new earth.

The heavens are vast in their array, with billions of stars, galaxies, solar systems, and planets. The Bible focuses, however, on the earth and how God is at work in our world. It tells the story of God's creation of the earth and humanity; of the problem of sin; and of how God redeems the world He created. Jesus said, "God so loved the world that he gave his one and only Son, that whoever believes in him shall not perish but have eternal life" (John 3:16). God so loved the world—the people and the planet—that He sent Jesus to save the world He created.

Norman Vincent Peale, pastor and author of the bestselling book *The Power of Positive Thinking,* shared a story about heaven that the widow of Thomas Edison, the great inventor, had shared with him. When Edison was in the last hours of his life, he was trying to say something. His doctor and his wife listened attentively as he struggled to speak. Then his doctor heard Edison whisper his last words: "It's very beautiful over there."[2]

God Is in Control

There is a cult of environmental fervor called Gaia that reveres Mother Earth as a deity and source of life. Spiritual feminism advocates a goddess (not God the Father) with feminine qualities that must replace the ostensibly violent, competitive, patriarchal style that dominates the marketplace. Ecology, for some, has become idolatry. "They exchanged the truth about God for a lie, and worshiped and served created things rather than the Creator—who is forever praised" (Romans 1:25). God commands us, "You shall have no other gods before me" (Exodus 20:3)—and that includes the planet.

Humanity is still trying to build the city of man without the city of God, as Augustine, the early Church leader, observed in his classic work *The City of God*, written around AD 413–426. In Fyodor Dostoevsky's last novel, *The Brothers Karamazov*, the fictional character Ivan Karamazov says, "If God does not exist, everything is permitted."[3]

The story is told that when British statesman Lord Gladstone visited Christ Church College and spoke with optimism about the betterment of society, a student asked him if anything concerned him about the world. He replied, "Yes, there is one thing that frightens me—the fear that God seems to be dying out of the minds of men."[4]

When I was a teenager, my pastor made the comment that the greatest challenge Christians face is living a spiritual life in a secular world. Secularism is the slow, gradual process by which faith and religious observance are constantly weakened. The United States, described as a Christian nation in an 1892 Supreme Court decision, has witnessed a great erosion of her spiritual and moral foundation in Judeo-Christian ethics.

The nation that prints on its currency, "In God We Trust," seldom mentions God in public life. Secular culture suppresses both the private belief in God and the public expression of faith.

Such was the concern of the prophet Jeremiah. He brought God's challenge to his generation:

"Has a nation ever changed its gods? (Yet they are not gods at all.) But my people have exchanged their glorious God for worthless idols. . . . Does a young woman forget her jewelry, a bride her wedding ornaments? Yet my people have forgotten me, days without number."

Jeremiah 2:11, 32

The revelation of God in Scripture begins with one foundational truth upon which our faith rests: "In the beginning God created the heavens and the earth" (Genesis 1:1). God exists independent of any cause; He is self-existent, the Creator of the universe, and the Author of life. "From him and through him and for him are all things. To him be the glory forever! Amen" (Romans 11:36).

God alone controls the universe. "The earth is the LORD's, and everything in it" (Psalm 24:1). God holds the universe together, "sustaining all things by his powerful word" (Hebrews 1:3). He causes the planets to rotate in order. He sustains the laws of physics and chemistry. He maintains the delicate balance of oxygen, nitrogen, and other gases, sustaining life on earth. God causes our hearts to beat, our lungs to breathe, and our brains to send impulses to our bodies' vital organs. God causes the sun to rise, so that morning brings us word of His unfailing love. "Now to the King eternal, immortal, invisible, the only God, be honor and glory for ever and ever. Amen" (1 Timothy 1:17).

Earth's Extravagance

The majesty of the earth was described by astronaut Jim Lovell of Apollo 8 to Mission Control hours after he and the crew viewed the first earthrise in December 1968 from one

Global Warming

of their orbits around the moon. He said, "The earth from here is a grand oasis in the big vastness of space."[5]

The Apollo 8 crew of Jim Lovell, Frank Borman, and Bill Anders ended their Christmas Eve television broadcast from space by reading the words of the Bible: "In the beginning God created the heavens and the earth." Each member took turns reading the creation story from the book of Genesis as the whole world listened. It was said that the broadcast provided a peaceful benediction to turbulent 1968 and saved the year.[6]

Frank Borman, commander of the mission, concluded the broadcast: "And from the crew of Apollo 8, we close with good night, good luck, a merry Christmas, and God bless all of you—all of you on the good earth."[7]

In a modern delusion called Deep Ecology, people worship the elements of the earth like ancient pagans. They believe the earth is our source of life, instead of the God who created the world. But the earth is the artwork of our Creator. The only way to appreciate a beautiful work of art is to highly esteem the artist. And the creation of the earth and heavens reveals what we need to know about the existence and nature of God:

> Since the creation of the world God's invisible qualities—his eternal power and divine nature—have been clearly seen, being understood from what has been made, so that people are without excuse.
>
> Romans 1:20

When you make a careful observation of our world, you see God in what He has made. You have no excuse, says Paul, not to believe in God. There exists far more evidence that God exists than that He does not exist. Demonstrating that God exists is easy based on the preponderance of evidence in creation, while there is no evidence that God does not exist.

Paul and Barnabas told the superstitious people at Lystra, who believed in Greek mythology, that God testifies to His existence in creation:

> "We are bringing you good news, telling you to turn from these worthless things to the living God, who made the heavens and the earth and the sea and everything in them. In the past, he let all nations go their own way. *Yet [God] has not left himself without testimony*: He has shown kindness by giving you rain from heaven and crops in their seasons; he provides you with plenty of food and fills your hearts with joy."
>
> Acts 14:15–17, emphasis added

Nature Testifies

The majesty of the mountains reveals God as El Shaddai, God Almighty, the God of the mountains; and as Jehovah Jireh: "On the mountain of the LORD it will be provided" (Genesis 22:14). Many people have died trying to climb Mount Everest because they lack the fear, reverence, and caution necessary to ascend to the summit. The mountains testify to the awe of God by which we should live: "You must still stand in awe of God" (Ecclesiastes 5:7 GNT).

The seven seas and the mighty rivers and streams all speak of the Holy Spirit. I once stood on the bank of mighty Mississippi River near its headwater in Minnesota and was awed by its power, swift current, and the loud sound of the rushing waters. I thought of Jesus' words:

Global Warming

"Let anyone who is thirsty come to me and drink. Whoever believes in me, as Scripture has said, rivers of living water will flow from within them." By this he meant the Spirit, whom those who believed in him were later to receive.

John 7:37–39

When John saw the risen Christ, he said, "His voice was like the sound of rushing waters" (Revelation 1:15).

Rain speaks to us of the Holy Spirit, who refreshes, renews, and revives us. God promises, "I will pour water on the thirsty land, and streams on the dry ground; I will pour out my Spirit on your offspring, and my blessing on your descendants" (Isaiah 44:3).

Forest fires, earthquakes, and tornadoes reveal the mighty power of God. When Moses climbed Mount Sinai to receive the Ten Commandments, God sent thunder and lightning, smoke on the mountain, and a loud trumpet blast (see Exodus 20:18). When God revealed Himself to Elijah at Mount Horeb, God sent a powerful wind, an earthquake, and a fire to get his attention. Then the prophet heard the still, small voice of God (see 1 Kings 19:12). From God's throne come "peals of thunder, rumblings, flashes of lightning and an earthquake" (Revelation 8:5).

Storms at sea describe a troubled world in need of redemption: "The wicked are like the tossing sea, which cannot rest, whose waves cast up mire and mud. 'There is no peace,' says my God, 'for the wicked'" (Isaiah 57:20–21). Yet Jesus, caught in a life-threatening storm, "got up, rebuked the wind and said to the waves, 'Quiet! Be still!' Then the wind died down and it was completely calm" (Mark 4:39). The disciples, terrified, asked, "Who is this? Even the wind and the waves obey him!" (verse 41). And Jesus is the One who can calm the troubled sea of the human heart.

The four winds of the heavens speak of the mysterious movement of the Holy Spirit. Jesus told Nicodemus:

> "You should not be surprised at my saying, 'You must be born again.' The wind blows wherever it pleases. You hear its sound, but you cannot tell where it comes from or where it is going. So it is with everyone born of the Spirit."
>
> John 3:7–8

The winds also remind us that one day Christ will gather His people home when He returns. "He will send his angels with a loud trumpet call, and they will gather his elect from the four winds, from one end of the heavens to the other" (Matthew 24:31).

The majestic clouds in the sky remind us that Jesus is coming again. "Then will appear the sign of the Son of Man in heaven. And then all the peoples of the earth will mourn when they see the Son of Man coming on the clouds of heaven, with power and great glory" (Matthew 24:30–31). John the Revelator writes: "'Look, he is coming with the clouds,' and 'every eye will see him'" (Revelation 1:7).

Every cloudy day should make us look up in expectation of our Lord's return, and remember that He reigns in heaven as our great High Priest and Lord of all.

Lessons from Nature

Nature teaches us powerful lessons about life if we look and learn. The animals give us insight into God's wisdom for our lives. "Ask the animals, and they will teach you, or the birds in the sky, and they will tell you" (Job 12:7).

Global Warming

The ants teach us to work: "Go to the ant, you sluggard; consider its ways and be wise!" (Proverbs 6:6). The lion teaches us courage: "The wicked flee though no one pursues, but the righteous are as bold as a lion" (Proverbs 28:1). The eagle teaches us to soar high: "Those who hope in the LORD . . . will soar on wings like eagles" (Isaiah 40:31). The birds teach us to trust God instead of worrying: "Look at the birds of the air; they do not sow or reap or store away in barns, and yet your heavenly Father feeds them" (Matthew 6:26).

The agriculture of the world describes the qualities of the Kingdom of God: "It is like a mustard seed, which is the smallest of all seeds on earth. Yet when planted, it grows and becomes the largest of all garden plants, with such big branches that the birds can perch in its shade" (Mark 4:31–32).

The flowers of the field remind us that God cares:

> "Why do you worry about clothes? See how the flowers of the field grow. They do not labor or spin. Yet I tell you that not even Solomon in all his splendor was dressed like one of these. If that is how God clothes the grass of the field . . . will he not much more clothe you—you of little faith?"
>
> Matthew 6:28–30

When I drove into Lompoc, California, to preach a revival at a church, I saw thousands of acres of beautiful flowers in full bloom. As a young man from Atlanta, I had never seen anything so beautiful. It was the harvest season, and the flower industry is a major part of their economy.

I grew up in a quiet neighborhood in south Atlanta. At evening people would often mow their lawns. The fragrance of fresh-cut grass in our neighborhood provided an incredible aroma. You could make perfume with the scent and call it Southern Fescue Fragrance! The grass of the world teaches us about life: "All people are like grass, and all their glory is like the flowers of the field; the grass withers and the flowers fall, but the word of the Lord endures forever" (1 Peter 1:24–25).

The fish of the sea describe humanity in need of the saving grace of God in Christ: "The kingdom of heaven is like a net that was let down into the lake and caught all kinds of fish. When it was full, the fishermen pulled it up on the shore" (Matthew 13:47–48). Jesus sends us out as fishermen: "I will send you out to fish for people" (Matthew 4:19). The Gospel of Christ is the net we cast into the sea of humanity to rescue as many as we can from the raging waters of sin and bring them safely to the shore of salvation.

I have been on a couple of fishing trips with men from our church. I am an awful fisherman, and I find fishing the most boring sport in the world. It is not a pastime, as some people call it, because time stands still when you go fishing! I prefer running, biking, or basketball for sport. But I want to be a skilled fisherman of people to catch them for Christ. I am confident that you share the same desire to be a fisherman of your family and friends.

Here is my point: Everything in this world teaches us about God. He created the world, and He takes care of it. So we do not need to worry about the planet because it belongs to God. Again: "The earth is the LORD's and everything in it" (Psalm 24:1). God will not terminate the world and neither will we. He will, however, transform the world when Christ returns to make a new earth!

The Faithful Witness in the Sky

The moon is earth's only natural satellite. The moon has been called our only constant cosmic companion. It makes the earth a more livable planet by stabilizing the earth's wobble on its axis, thus creating a stable climate. The moon also causes tides, creating a rhythm that has guided humans for thousands of years in sea travel.

The diameter of the moon is roughly one-fourth that of the earth. It is covered with craters, mountains, and plains. It orbits the earth and revolves at the same rate every twenty-seven days. It is 238,855 miles away. Thirty earths could fit between us! Its core, like that of earth, is made of iron and nickel, creating a magnetic force with our planet. The moon appears to us in different ways—the new moon, full moon, harvest moon, blood moon, and more.

The moon is God's faithful witness to the inhabitants of the earth:

> "Once for all, I have sworn by my holiness—and I will not lie to David—that his line will continue forever and his throne endure before me like the sun; it will be established forever like the moon, the faithful witness in the sky."
>
> Psalm 89:35–37

The climate activists who promote false fear about the self-destruction of the planet need to know God's promise that the sun, moon, and earth are established forever. The earth will not be destroyed by global warming, nuclear war, or environmental disaster. God is faithful to care for the world He created. If the earth has endured for 4.5 billion years, and humanity has been here since around 10,000 BC, our planet is resilient and its people are resilient. God endowed us with the ability to adapt to climate change and to survive the severest storms and weather conditions.

So don't live in fear about the earth's future. God has it all under control. After the Flood, He assured Noah, "As long as the earth endures, seedtime and harvest, cold and heat, summer and winter, day and night will never cease" (Genesis 8:22). The earth moves naturally through climate and environmental cycles over time. Climate change is a normal part of the earth's patterns. Besides, God has plans to restore and renew the earth. And when Jesus returns, life on earth will change for the better!

As a child, I never thought about asking my father or mother to take care of me. I felt no anxiety about having a home in which to live, clothes to wear, or food to eat. I knew intuitively that they would take care of me because they had taken care of me from the moment I came into the world.

As God's kids, we can trust Him to provide for the planet and for His people, because He has proved His faithfulness from the moment He created the earth. Jesus said, "If you, then, though you are evil, know how to give good gifts to your children, how much more will your Father in heaven give good gifts to those who ask him!" (Matthew 7:11).

Take Care of the World

"The LORD God took the man and put him in the Garden of Eden to work it and take care of it" (Genesis 2:15). The law of success is found in those words *work it and take care of it*. If you do those two things in every area of your life, you will succeed! Work and care—those are the time-proven values of success.

Global Warming

The word *stewardship* means to carefully and conscientiously manage what God has entrusted to us. We need to optimize our opportunities. Never squander your time, talent, or treasure. "It is required that those who have been given a trust must prove faithful" (1 Corinthians 4:2). We cannot change every aspect of the earth's environment. Only God controls the weather. (If I could control the weather, it would never rain on Sunday!) And we cannot control the climate. But we can and should take care of the world God gave us.

Highways and streets often post signs reading *$500 Fine for Littering*. One day I went with my dad to a store and noticed a sign that read *No Loitering*. I asked him what the word *loitering* meant. He said, "It means that if you don't have money in your pocket, you shouldn't enter the store. You need to be here to buy something or shop for something, but not to hang out." Littering and loitering ruin the world, whereas work and care make the world a great place to live.

My first job was working at a new grocery store in our neighborhood during the summer. I showed up early my first day of work on Saturday at 8 a.m. The manager met me, then handed me a broom. He walked with me outside, looked at the curb and sidewalk, and explained the importance of a clean sidewalk when customers first arrive. "We start the day cleaning the outside of the store," he told me, "before people enter to shop."

This manager was teaching me (as my parents had always taught me) the first law of success: *Take care of what you have*. Take pride in the condition of everything—the way things look and the way things work.

When I drive by that same store today, it looks dirty and disorganized, for one reason—people stopped taking care of it. Appearance is the result of appreciation. When we appreciate something, we take care of it.

God created the world and gave it to us as our home, and He expects us to take care of it. If we take care of the planet, it will benefit us. When we mismanage the planet, we negatively impact our living conditions.

The law of sowing and reaping—we reap what we sow— also applies to our planet. While many people, especially young people, worry about climate change and the future of the planet, we should be working to take care of the earth as God intended when He put mankind in the Garden of Eden. If we work today, we don't have to worry about tomorrow.

Earth Day is observed every April 22 to emphasize our responsibility to care diligently for the planet God provided us. Human history will end and the real Earth Day will take place when God restores the earth to its original glory: "Then I saw 'a new heaven and a new earth'" (Revelation 21:1). Isaiah the prophet foresaw this new creation:

"See, I will create new heavens and a new earth. The former things will not be remembered, nor will they come to mind. But be glad and rejoice forever in what I will create, for I will create Jerusalem to be a delight and its people a joy."

Isaiah 65:17–18

The apostle Peter assures us: "In keeping with his promise we are looking forward to a new heaven and a new earth, where righteousness dwells" (2 Peter 3:13). While we look forward to the new world, it our responsibility today to be good stewards of the planet God gave us as our home.

ELEVEN

THE GOVERNMENT
OF GOD

After the atomic bombs were dropped to end World War II, Albert Einstein said, "The unleashed power of the atom has changed everything except our thinking. Thus, we are drifting toward catastrophe beyond conception. We shall require a substantially new manner of thinking if mankind is to survive." He added, "As long as armies exist, any serious quarrel will lead to war." Peace is not the absence of war, he noted, but the presence of justice.[1]

One day peace will come through the justice of God. When the Prince of Peace returns from heaven to reign as King of kings and Lord of lords, there will be peace. The Bible describes this new eternal age, as we have been discussing, as the Millennium—the thousand-year reign of Christ. His Kingdom is a Kingdom of righteousness and peace.

The Millennium is referred to in the Bible as "the last days" (Isaiah 2:2), "a day of the LORD" (Zechariah 14:1), "the kingdom of heaven" (Matthew 18:3), "the renewal of all things" (Matthew 19:28), "the times of restoration of all things" (Acts 3:21 NKJV), and "the age to come" (Hebrews 6:5 NKJV). We live in the present age of sin and suffering, but when Jesus Christ returns, we will live in the age to come of the peace and prosperity of God. What does the Bible tell us about the Millennium or the Kingdom age of Christ?

The word *millennium* means a thousand years and is used only in Revelation 20. Is the thousand years a literal time period? I suppose no one knows for sure. We know that numbers in the book of Revelation seldom mean only numbers; they represent spiritual truths. The number one thousand speaks of a golden age, a completed time in which God fulfills His plan. Whether or not a thousand is literal or figurative does not really matter. What matters is that Christ will rule as King of kings, and we will rule and reign with Him.

During the Last Supper, Jesus told the apostles, "I confer on you a kingdom, just as my Father conferred one on me, so that you may eat and drink at my table in my kingdom and sit on thrones, judging the twelve tribes of Israel" (Luke 22:29–30). Paul the apostle asked, "Do you not know that we will judge angels? How much more the things of this life!" (1 Corinthians 6:3). While we don't understand everything about the age to come, one truth is certain: We will reign with Christ!

John the apostle wrote:

I saw thrones on which were seated those who had been given authority to judge. And I saw the souls of those who had been beheaded because of their testimony about Jesus and because of the word of God. . . . They came to life and reigned with Christ a thousand years.

Revelation 20:4

The Government of God

Here we see three incredible promises: thrones for believers, the authority to judge, and reigning with Christ. Jesus promises, "To the one who is victorious, I will give the right to sit with me on my throne, just as I was victorious and sat down with my Father on his throne" (Revelation 3:21).

We cannot always trust the news to tell us what is really going on in the world. But while the world worries over fake news, we rejoice in faith news! The last chapter of history will be the return of Jesus Christ. When He returns, He will set up the Kingdom of God under His own kingly rule with righteousness and peace.

The Millennium is the fulfillment of the covenant God made with King David. The angel Gabriel, when he appeared to Mary to announce the Savior's birth, referenced the Davidic covenant. He said to Mary:

> "You will conceive and give birth to a son, and you are to call him Jesus. He will be great and will be called the Son of the Most High. The Lord God will give him the throne of his father David, and he will reign over Jacob's descendants forever; his kingdom will never end."
>
> Luke 1:31–33

The final government is the Kingdom of God on earth when Jesus returns in power and glory: "The kingdoms of this world have become the kingdoms of our Lord and of His Christ, and He shall reign forever and ever!" (Revelation 11:15 NKJV). When our Lord returns, God will fulfill His purpose in world history "to bring unity to all things in heaven and on earth under Christ" (Ephesians 1:10).

The Millennial reign of Jesus Christ will be an unparalleled time of peace and prosperity for the whole world. So don't be hopeless about the future—because the future is as bright as the promises of God!

Three Views of the Kingdom

Bible scholars hold different views about the nature, length, and purpose of the Millennium. Most importantly, we need to know that we live in the Kingdom of God now and that we will be part of Christ's eternal Kingdom in the age to come.

Amillennialism

Amillennialism takes the view that there is no literal Kingdom age of Christ and that the reference to a thousand years in Revelation 20:1–6 is figurative, descriptive of believers who have died and gone to heaven. Proponents of this view see the throne of Christ as His rule in heaven now, which believers share with Him.

But while we are promised heaven the moment the body dies and the soul is united with Christ, there also remains Jesus' promise to return to this world a second time. When people say that Jesus will not *literally* return, remember the words of Hebrews 9:28: "Christ was sacrificed once to take away the sins of many; and *he will appear a second time*, not to bear sin, but to bring salvation to those who are waiting for him" (emphasis added).

Postmillennialism

Postmillennialism is the view that the world will eventually be transformed into a Christian culture by the influence of the Church. Then, when we get the world straightened out, Jesus will return.

The Government of God

If that is true, we are a long way from Jesus' return, because the world is getting worse by the day. Besides, we cannot have the Kingdom without the King. So we pray, "Amen. Come, Lord Jesus" (Revelation 22:20). We cannot produce the Kingdom of God by trying to make politics, economics, commerce, education, entertainment, and the legal system conform to Christian standards.

While we should bring Christian values into the marketplace, government, school systems, and media platforms, that action alone will not transform the entire world into the Kingdom of God. We are the salt of the earth and the light of the world as witnesses of Christ. But we will still long for and look forward to the return of our Lord, who will remove evil and restore this world to God's perfect plan.

Premillennialism

Premillennialism teaches the biblical truth that Jesus will return to reign on earth as Lord of all. His return is the beginning of the age to come.

The early Church believed in the premillennial return of Jesus. Many centuries later, the other two positions, amillennialism and postmillennialism, appeared.

Politicians offer hope and change, but only Jesus can bring lasting hope to our world. Only when He comes will the Lord's Prayer be answered: "Your Kingdom come, Your will be done, on earth as it is in heaven." The Kingdom age under the rule of Christ will restore everything to divine order, from animals to agriculture, politics to pollution, education to economics. The quality of nature, relationships, and institutions when Jesus returns will be one of righteousness and peace.

187

World Conditions

What will the world be like after Jesus returns?

Politics

Will the nations of the world still be governed by liberals, conservatives, independents, and socialists? No, the nations will be governed by Jesus Christ, for God will "bring unity to all things in heaven and on earth under Christ" (Ephesians 1:10). Zechariah wrote: "The LORD will be king over the whole earth. On that day there will be one LORD, and his name the only name" (Zechariah 14:9).

The Millennium answers the exclamation of the crowd at Jesus' Triumphal Entry: "Blessed is the king who comes in the name of the Lord!" (Luke 19:38). Jesus' reign as the Son of David fulfills the Davidic covenant, in which God promised King David a *house*, a *throne*, and a *kingdom* for his descendants forever (see 2 Samuel 7:13).

Isaiah wrote of the Messiah:

> The government will be upon His shoulder. And His name will be called . . . Prince of Peace. Of the increase of His government and peace there will be no end, upon the throne of David and over His kingdom, to order it and establish it with judgment and justice from that time forward, even forever. The zeal of the LORD of hosts will perform this.
>
> Isaiah 9:6–7 NKJV

Environment

Isaiah describes the restoration of the animal kingdom as it was in the Garden of Eden before sin entered the world:

The Government of God

The wolf will live with the lamb, the leopard will lie down with the goat, the calf and the lion and the yearling together; and a little child will lead them. The cow will feed with the bear, their young will lie down together, and the lion will eat straw like the ox. The infant will play near the cobra's den, and the young child will put its hand into the viper's nest.

Isaiah 11:6–8

Zechariah describes the environment of the Millennium:

On that day there will be neither sunlight nor cold, frosty darkness. It will be a unique day—a day known only to the LORD—with no distinction between day and night. When evening comes, there will be light. On that day living water will flow out from Jerusalem, half of it east to the Dead Sea and half of it west to the Mediterranean Sea, in summer and in winter.

Zechariah 14:6–8

No more climate change or global warming hysteria. No more hurricanes, tornadoes, or tsunamis. The weather in the new world will be perfect every day.

Peace

The prevailing atmosphere will be righteousness and peace. The Revelator said the devil will be bound in the abyss for a thousand years (see Revelation 20:2), which means that evil will be held back.

All the problems in our world are, first and foremost, spiritual problems, and are corrected by righteousness and peace. When things are right in God's eyes, we have peace. All relationships in families, nations, and societies will be governed by righteousness and peace. Violence will end. Wars will cease. Poverty will vanish. Injustice will end. It will be a time of unparalleled prosperity. Such is the world to come when Christ returns.

The social turmoil in the world stems from ungodly and foolish leaders. "The wicked are like the tossing sea, which cannot rest, whose waves cast up mire and mud. 'There is no peace,' says my God, 'for the wicked'" (Isaiah 57:20–21). The popular phrase "Elections have consequences" is accurate. World conflicts, high inflation, suppression of free speech, failing educational systems, lawlessness, rising crime, rampant immorality—all come from the sin nature. Jesus said, "Every good tree bears good fruit, but a bad tree bears bad fruit" (Matthew 7:17). Bad-natured politicians enact bad policies, which make life bad for people. "When the righteous are in authority, the people rejoice; but when a wicked man rules, the people groan" (Proverbs 29:2 NKJV).

The armies of the world will lay down their weapons:

> They will beat their swords into plowshares and their spears into pruning hooks. Nation will not take up sword against nation, nor will they train for war anymore. . . . The earth will be filled with the knowledge of the LORD as the waters cover the sea.
>
> Isaiah 2:4; 11:9

The Prince of Peace will teach the nations of the world how to walk in the light of His love.

Law

In the Millennium, the law of God will govern the world. The words *righteousness* and *peace* describe the quality of

The Government of God

life in the Kingdom of God. These two words are often found together in the Bible. Righteousness comes first, then peace, because peace is the result of righteousness. When things are right, they are peaceful. "Since we have been justified [made righteous] through faith, we have peace with God through our Lord Jesus Christ" (Romans 5:1).

Isaiah writes, "The fruit of that righteousness will be peace; its effect will be quietness and confidence forever" (Isaiah 32:17). The Kingdom of God is "righteousness, peace and joy in the Holy Spirit" (Romans 14:17). James reassures us that "peacemakers who sow in peace reap a harvest of righteousness" (James 3:18). Jesus, like the Old Testament priest Melchizedek, is the King of righteousness and the King of peace (see Hebrews 7:1–2).

The Church of Jesus Christ constitutes the Kingdom of God on earth. When we live in righteousness and peace, we show others the higher standard of life they can find in Christ, the more excellent way to live. The politics, protests, and provocations that trigger chaos in our world are created by unrighteousness. When righteousness reigns, peace also reigns. The work of righteousness is always peace. When we work for liberty and justice in the right way, peace will come.

Ethics

Today we battle moral relativism. The cry of the age is: Whatever feels good, do it! Ethics are situational. But in the Kingdom age, the prevailing moral climate will be holiness. Isaiah saw a great highway of holiness in the Millennium (see Isaiah 35:8–10). Can you image interstate signs reading "Highway of Holiness"? If we drove with holiness, there would be no road rage! Holiness means to be special, sacred, and dedicated to God for His purposes. We live all of life for God's glory.

Zechariah wrote that holiness means living as the special people of God:

> On that day HOLY TO THE LORD will be inscribed on the bells of the horses, and the cooking pots in the LORD's house will be like the sacred bowls in front of the altar. Every pot in Jerusalem and Judah will be holy to the LORD Almighty.
>
> Zechariah 14:20–21

Maybe we will have license plates on our cars with that inscription. Zechariah said that *Holiness* will even be inscribed on the pots and pans. Holiness will be our standard of living, right down to the daily stuff of life in the age to come.

Worship

During the Millennium, world religions and secular philosophies will go by the wayside, as everyone will worship the living God "in the Spirit and in truth," as Jesus said (John 4:23). All will confess that Jesus is Lord. As Isaiah wrote:

> Many peoples will come and say, "Come, let us go up to the mountain of the LORD, to the temple of the God of Jacob. He will teach us his ways, so that we may walk in his paths." The law will go out from Zion, the word of the LORD from Jerusalem.
>
> Isaiah 2:3

The Government of God

And Zechariah wrote:

> The LORD will be king over the whole earth. On that day there will be one LORD, and his name the only name. . . . Then the survivors from all the nations that have attacked Jerusalem will go up year after year to worship the King, the LORD Almighty.
>
> Zechariah 14:9, 16

A person can live forty days without food, twelve days without sleep, and six days without water. But how long can a person live without hope? God is the God of hope. Bible prophecy gives us hope for both the present age and also the age to come.

Jesus' return gives us hope for the future: "We wait for the blessed hope—the appearing of the glory of our great God and Savior, Jesus Christ" (Titus 2:13). God will give you hope today if you trust Him with your life. Your greatest hope is the promise of eternal life, because you have put your faith in Jesus as your Savior.

The Kingdom Now

It takes a lot of time and effort to earn citizenship in the United States. I have attended several celebrations in which family members received their citizenship. New citizens are always proud, cherishing the privilege of being part of a free nation.

Our citizenship in the Kingdom of God takes no work or time. You don't have to wait until Jesus returns to live in the Kingdom of God and experience righteousness and peace. You can be a citizen of the Kingdom of God now. When you put your faith in Jesus Christ and confess that Jesus is Lord, you become a citizen of heaven. Jesus said, "The kingdom of God has come near. Repent and believe the good news!" (Mark 1:15).

When you receive Christ as your Savior, a kingdom transfer occurs in your life: "He has rescued us from the dominion of darkness and brought us into the kingdom of the Son he loves, in whom we have redemption, the forgiveness of sins" (Colossians 1:13–14). Every Christian is given a new citizenship. "Our citizenship is in heaven" (Philippians 3:20). Christian citizenship is a gift from God.

> When the kindness and love of God our Savior appeared, he saved us, not because of righteous things we had done, but because of his mercy. He saved us through the washing of rebirth and renewal by the Holy Spirit, whom he poured out on us generously through Jesus Christ our Savior.
>
> Titus 3:4–6

Final Outcome

Are you ready for eternity? Remember your final destiny: "People are destined to die once, and after that to face judgment" (Hebrews 9:27). The word *judgment* means to be examined, evaluated, and appraised. We will be judged for our actions. "The dead were judged according to what they had done as recorded in the books" (Revelation 20:12). Judgment involves personal responsibility, for "each of us will give an account of ourselves to God" (Romans 14:12). That is something we all share—after this life, the judgment.

We will also be judged for our response to Jesus. When Pilate questioned Jesus, he told the crowd, "I find no fault in

The Government of God

him!" (John 19:4). Then he asked the most important question of life: "What shall I do . . . with Jesus who is called the Messiah?" (Matthew 27:22). A person can either receive or reject Jesus, once he or she experiences a revelation of Christ. "To all who did receive him, to those who believed in his name, he gave the right to become children of God" (John 1:12).

Before you go to dinner at a restaurant, you make a reservation. In the same way, you need to make your reservation for heaven by receiving Jesus as your Savior. When you do, your name is written in the Book of Life. Jesus said, "Rejoice that your names are written in heaven" (Luke 10:20). At the final judgment, John wrote, "I saw the dead, great and small, standing before the throne, and books were opened. Another book was opened, which is the book of life" (Revelation 20:12). Only those whose names are recorded in the Book of Life are saved for eternity. Your good works recorded in the books cannot save you—only your name recorded in the Book of Life.

It is my prayer for you that you will receive Jesus Christ as your Savior and know that your name is written in heaven.

TWELVE

A SKEPTIC'S GUIDE TO FAITH

I have discovered a growing skepticism among some believers regarding the Second Coming of Christ. They have forgotten that Jesus promised to return. Perhaps we have been numbed to our Lord's promise by sensational prophecy preachers, dramatic movies, books about the Rapture, and hysterical predictions regarding pandemics, natural disasters, blood moons, the appearance of comets, and political change. Sensationalism breeds skepticism because these predictions never come to pass.

One afternoon when I was a boy, I was playing in the backyard by myself. I wanted my mother's attention, so I called for her to come outside, saying I felt sick. She came out and checked on me and said, "David, you're fine. You're not sick." A little later I called for her to help me because I had fallen down and was hurt. She came running out of house, only to discover I was fine. At that point she must have realized I was just trying to get her attention.

We had a stone wall around the back of the house that contained a large flower bed. My dad had built the stone wall just for her. She loved to grow plants and flowers all around our house. She sat down with me on the stone wall and said, "David, I want to tell you a story." (I was loving the attention I was getting from her at that point.)

She proceeded to tell me one of Aesop's fables about the boy who cried wolf.

One day, as my mother told the story, a shepherd boy was tending a flock of sheep outside the village. He decided to play a trick on the villagers, so he cried out, "Wolf! Wolf!"

The men ran out of the village to help him, only to discover there was no wolf.

"Don't cry wolf," they told him, "when there is no wolf!"

But the boy laughed at the sight of their angry faces.

Later that day he cried out again, "Wolf! Wolf!"

Again the men of the village rushed to drive the wolf away, only to find there was no wolf. Again they rebuked him.

But the boy chuckled with delight at their naïveté.

That evening a wolf came and scattered the herd.

"Wolf! Wolf!" the boy cried desperately. But no one came.

When darkness came and the boy had not returned to the village, the men in the town went out to search for him and found the boy looking frantically for the sheep.

"A wolf came," cried the boy, "and the sheep ran away from the wolf, and I can't find them. I cried for help, but no one came."

As they walked back to the village together, an old man comforted the boy.

A Skeptic's Guide to Faith

"We'll help you look for the lost sheep in the morning," he said, putting his arm around the youth. "Nobody believes a liar, even when he is telling the truth."

Unfortunately, after my mother told me that story, I did not know what it meant. But I was so afraid that a wolf would come out of the woods behind our house and eat me that I never called for my mother again just for attention that day!

Modern-day preachers who cry, "Christ is coming! Christ is coming!" in response to every political uprising, environmental disaster, terrorist attack, or heavenly sign like a blood moon or comet are like the boy who cried wolf. So stop listening to their hysteria and put your faith in Jesus, who said, "About that day or hour no one knows, not even the angels in heaven, nor the Son, but only the Father" (Matthew 24:36). The most important thing is to be watchful, ready, and faithful to meet Him when He appears.

Delayed Promise

I often hear believers lament the conditions of the world and ask, "Why does Jesus delay His return?" We often look up to heaven and pray, "Come, Lord Jesus!"

Two things I have learned about God: You cannot hurry Him and you cannot hinder Him. When God acts in His perfect time, it is swift and decisive. So it will be when He opens the heavens for His Son to return, "coming on the clouds of heaven, with power and great glory" (Matthew 24:30).

Bible prophecy is given to educate, encourage, and equip us, not to entertain us. The promise of Jesus' coming should empower us to proclaim the Gospel to a world in need of His saving grace. Jesus told the disciples before His ascension:

"It is not for you to know the times or dates the Father has set by his own authority. But you will receive power when the Holy Spirit comes on you; and you will be my witnesses" (Acts 1:7–8). The word *set* means predetermined or predestined. The times and dates of Jesus' Second Coming are predestined by God. What we need is power for the present, not predictions about the future.

Jesus also said, "As lightning that comes from the east is visible even in the west, so will be the coming of the Son of Man" (Matthew 24:27). He will come like a thief in the night (see Matthew 24:43).

The last words of Jesus recorded in the Bible are, "Yes, I am coming soon" (Revelation 22:20). The word *yes* means He is faithful to keep His promise. Jesus has delayed His return for some two thousand years, but His promise to return is certain. When He finished giving the prophetic signs of His coming, signs we have discussed earlier in this book, He said, "Heaven and earth will pass away, but my words will never pass away" (Matthew 24:35).

The apostle Peter reminds us that Jesus' return is guaranteed:

You must understand that in the last days scoffers will come, scoffing and following their own evil desires. They will say, "Where is this 'coming' he promised? Ever since our ancestors died, everything goes on as it has since the beginning of creation." But they deliberately forget that long ago by God's word the heavens came into being and the earth was formed out of water and by water. By these waters also the world of that time was deluged and destroyed. By the same word the present heavens and earth are reserved for fire, being kept for the day of judgment and destruction of the ungodly.

But do not forget this one thing, dear friends: With the Lord a day is like a thousand years, and a thousand years are like a day. The Lord is not slow in keeping his promise, as some understand slowness. Instead he is patient with you, not wanting anyone to perish, but everyone to come to repentance.

But the day of the Lord will come like a thief.

2 Peter 3:3–10

Doubting Disciples

Given the certainty of Jesus' promise, what a tragedy to see some Christians doubt Christ's return! What a paradox—doubting disciples! Such Christians are a walking contradiction.

I certainly don't know everything about prophecy and the end of the age, but one thing is for certain—I don't doubt Christ's promise to return to this earth with power and glory, to be hailed as King of kings and Lord of lords. I don't know how and when He will return, but I believe His promise.

God's promises don't have to pass the test of our limited knowledge to be true. First and foremost is Jesus' promise to come back and make all things new. Peter wrote that "in keeping with his promise we are looking forward to a new heaven and a new earth, where righteousness dwells" (2 Peter 3:13).

When my parents promised to do something for me, I did not ask them for proof. I certainly did not ask them to give me a sign. I trusted my parents because they proved their love and faithfulness every moment of my life. When they made a promise, I knew beyond the shadow of a doubt that their word was true. How much greater is the promise of Christ to us when He says, "I will come back and take you to be with me that you also may be where I am" (John 14:3)? Where is Jesus today? He is in heaven, and He will come back from heaven to this world at the end of this age.

After Jesus' resurrection, some of His disciples who saw the risen Lord still doubted. Matthew tells us of one of the last times Jesus appeared to them before He returned to heaven: "The eleven disciples went to Galilee, to the mountain where Jesus had told them to go. When they saw him, they worshiped him; *but some doubted*" (Matthew 28:16–17, emphasis added).

The disciples gathered with Jesus at the Mount of Olives and worshiped Him. This was the last time they would see Jesus. They saw the nail prints in His hands and feet. They had seen the wound in His side from the soldier's spear. They had eaten with the risen Lord. Jesus had spent forty days with them after His resurrection, teaching them about the Kingdom of God and preparing them to go into all the world and make disciples. Yet some doubted?

Yes, there were doubting disciples. There were faithless followers.

So I say to you who are skeptical about Jesus' return, saying that it is merely symbolic, not literal: You need to doubt your doubts and be skeptical of your skepticism and believe what Jesus said: "I am coming soon!"

When the skeptics of this age debunk the promise of Christ's return, hold fast to Jesus' promise. Doubt the skeptics but don't ever doubt the Savior!

Paul clarifies the final outcome of world history and explains how God is working out His plan:

> He made known to us the mystery of his will according to his good pleasure, which he purposed in Christ, to be put

into effect when the times reach their fulfillment—to bring unity to all things in heaven and on earth under Christ.

Ephesians 1:9–10

The end of this age is the beginning of a new eternal age. Our souls are eternal. "We will be with the Lord forever. Therefore encourage one another with these words" (1 Thessalonians 4:17–18).

Homeward Bound

One of my favorite movies is *Homeward Bound*, which features two dogs and a cat that traveled three hundred miles to get back home and be reunited with their family. We, too, are homeward bound for eternity!

I have already shared with you about the new earth God will create. But when we read that Jesus also promised "a new heaven," it raises questions. What is heaven? Where is heaven?

I don't get lost in the details about heaven, since we see through the glass dimly. I simply think of heaven as eternal life with God. Jesus said:

> "Do not let your hearts be troubled. You believe in God; believe also in me. My Father's house has many rooms; if that were not so, would I have told you that I am going there to prepare a place for you? And if I go and prepare a place for you, I will come back and take you to be with me that you also may be where I am."

John 14:1–3

The secular person believes only in this world. Ralph Waldo Emerson wrote, "Other world! there is no other world. God is one and omnipresent; here or nowhere is the whole fact."[1]

Former Beatle John Lennon penned the hopeless words to the otherwise beautiful song "Imagine" to describe the secular view: "Imagine there's no heaven. . . ." I am a songwriter with many published songs, but if I rewrote that song, I would sing, "Imagine there's a heaven. . . ."

Jesus made it easy for us to imagine heaven with His words, "In My Father's house are many mansions" (John 14:2 NKJV). Heaven is a place of mansions, or elaborate rooms, like the greatest luxury hotel in the world, or an exquisite palace in the countryside, or a plush penthouse apartment overlooking the cityscape. Use your imagination!

Every morning when I leave for work, I tell my miniature long-haired dachshunds, Mikey and Beau, "I've got to go to work now. I'll be back. Watch the house till I get home." They seem to know exactly what I mean because they get into their beds as if to say, "We'll be here waiting for you." When I get home, they greet me at the door, jumping up and down, spinning like tops, tongues and tails wagging, and barking loudly as if to say, "We've been watching and waiting for you to come back home!"

Jesus left this world for heaven. He told us He is preparing a place for us. He assured us that He will come back for us. So we need to watch and wait for Him to return. We also need to do the work He assigned to us.

Research indicates that nearly 80 percent of Americans believe in life after death, and two-thirds are certain there is a heaven. Although some other religions believe in heaven or paradise, the Bible is the only definitive textbook on the subject of heaven.

A Skeptic's Guide to Faith

The term *heaven* is used three ways in Scripture. First, there is the natural atmosphere that surrounds the earth. Second, there is the spiritual, heavenly realm of angels and demons. In Paul's letter to the Ephesians, he mentions the heavenly realms five times. For example, in Ephesians 2:6 he says we are seated with Christ in the heavenly realms, and in Ephesians 6:12 he says that we struggle "against the spiritual forces of evil in the heavenly realms." Third, heaven is the dwelling of God. Paul says he "was caught up to the third heaven" and "heard inexpressible things, things that no one is permitted to tell" (2 Corinthians 12:2, 4).

The four gospels contain more than one hundred references to heaven; and Jesus spoke often about the Kingdom of heaven. He taught us to pray, "Your will be done on earth as it is in heaven" (Matthew 6:10).

Bishop Fulton Sheen was scheduled to speak in Philadelphia at Town Hall. He decided to walk from his hotel even though he was unfamiliar with the city. Sure enough, he got lost and stopped to ask some boys playing in the street how to get there. The boys asked, "What are you going to do there?"

He replied, "I'm going to give a lecture."

"On what?" the boys asked.

Bishop Sheen said, "I'm going to talk on Heaven and how to get there. Would you like to come and find out?"

The boys scoffed. "You don't even know the way to the Town Hall!"[2]

How Do We Get to Heaven?

When Jesus told His disciples He was going away to prepare a place for them, He added, "You know the way to the place

I am going." He was saying, "You know the way to heaven." But Thomas replied, "Lord, we don't even know where You are going, so how can we get there?"

Then Jesus gave the most comforting and controversial statement He ever made: "I am the way and the truth and the life. No one comes to the Father except through me" (John 14:6).

One distinguishing feature of the Christian faith that separates it from all other religions is the fact that Jesus promised us eternal life. Jesus is the only religious leader in history to guarantee people who believed in Him eternal life. He said, "Most assuredly, I say to you, he who believes in Me has everlasting life" (John 6:47 NKJV).

Jesus is the way to heaven. When you believe in Jesus as your Savior, you have eternal life.

John the apostle ended his first letter with a note of assurance: "I write these things to you who believe in the name of the Son of God so that you may know that you have eternal life" (1 John 5:13).

I accepted Christ when I was about eight years old. Later, when I was worried about my salvation, my mother showed me that verse of Scripture—so that I would know that I had eternal life. I have never doubted my salvation since. You can know that you have eternal life today when you trust Christ to save you from your sins and give you the gift of eternal life. "This is what he promised us—eternal life" (1 John 2:25).

Following a Christmas message for a community group, a woman asked me how she could share her faith with her elderly father, who was an atheist. He had told her recently that he wondered where he would go after he died. So she asked me, "Where will he go?"

I told her that I am not in the place of God, so I don't know anyone's eternal destiny. I do, however, know the way to heaven through Jesus Christ, because only Christ promises us eternal life. Jesus alone has provided a way to God through His atoning sacrifice on the cross, His glorious resurrection, and His triumphant ascension to heaven as our Savior and Lord.

Then this woman asked, "What would you say if an atheist asked you where he would go when he dies?"

"The first thing I would ask him," I replied, "is why he is so concerned about eternity if he doesn't believe in God."

That is a contradiction—an atheist worrying about where he will spend eternity! Why worry about something you don't believe in?

Perhaps her father had more faith than he thought he had. He obviously did not believe his atheism. Atheism, you see, is just as much of a religion as any other faith or lack of faith. Believing in nothing takes as much effort as believing in something. In fact, believing in nothing is more difficult because we are surrounded by so much evidence of God. It is far easier to demonstrate that God exists than that He does not exist. We are all believers. We either believe in something or in nothing. But there are no nonbelievers. Atheism can be a cover-up of deeper spiritual issues in a person's heart such as disappointment with religion, spiritual confusion, or anger toward God regarding suffering.

I suggested that this woman ask her father why he was worried about life after death. Where did his worry come from? He might realize that his concern about eternity came from his own heart, because God was dealing with him about his soul. His mind had discounted God, but his heart was convicting him, telling him that he needed a relationship with God; and until he had that relationship, he would not be at peace. If his atheism had brought him anxiety, perhaps it was time for him to take Jesus' advice—"Stop doubting and believe" (John 20:27)—and exchange his atheism for assurance in Christ.

I suggested she ask her father where he *wanted* to go when he died. If he said heaven, then she could tell him he could get there if he trusted Christ to save him from his sins and give him eternal life.

Only the One who came from heaven can take us to heaven. Jesus is the only One who has ever graced the stage of human history and guaranteed eternal life to those who believe in Him. Jesus is the way to heaven. Trust Him and you will have eternal life.

Living with Hope

Christ is coming—so what? What difference does His return make in our lives today?

What we believe about the future has a profound impact on us today. For example, if you were sick and diagnosed with a dreaded disease and a poor prognosis, you might lose all hope and get your house in order, to prepare for your end. When the future looks bleak, people become hopeless. But if you were cured of that disease and then assured that you would live a long time, you would begin to dream about the things you looked forward to doing. When the future is bright, people have hope!

The purpose of Bible prophecy is to give us hope for the future. As Paul the apostle said, "If only for this life we have hope in Christ, we are of all people most to be pitied"

(1 Corinthians 15:19). This is why Titus called the promise of Christ's return "the blessed hope—the appearing of the glory of our great God and Savior, Jesus Christ" (Titus 2:13). His coming is our happy hope!

The apostle Peter gave us a great challenge in view of Christ's return: "What kind of people ought you to be? You ought to live holy and godly lives as you look forward to the day of God and speed its coming" (2 Peter 3:11–12).

God does not reveal the future merely to give us information but to give us inspiration and instruction. As the people of God who know the outcome of history, we should live holy, hopeful, and hurried lives.

Holy Lives

God calls us to be a holy people. We live in the world, but we are not of the world. The word *holy* means special, unique, and dedicated to God for His purposes.

We are "a chosen people, a royal priesthood, a holy nation, God's special possession" (1 Peter 2:9). God calls us to holiness: "Be holy, because I am holy" (1 Peter 1:16). Holiness pleases God. "It is God's will that you should be sanctified" (1 Thessalonians 4:3). *Sanctified* means set apart. Holiness should be our pursuit: "Make every effort to live in peace with everyone and to be holy; without holiness no one will see the Lord" (Hebrews 12:14).

We are also called to be godly. Godliness simply means to be like God. Since He is our Father, and since most children emulate their parents, we need to emulate Him. The greatest way to be like God is to love others, for God is love: "Be imitators of God as dear children. And walk in love" (Ephesians 5:1–2 NKJV). If we truly believe that Jesus is coming again, then our lives will reflect that faith. "When Christ appears, we shall be like him, for we shall see him as he is. All who have this hope in him purify themselves, just as he is pure" (1 John 3:2–3).

The promise of the Second Coming of Jesus has a profound effect on us as His disciples to live holy and godly lives for His glory, "so that when he appears we may be confident and unashamed before him at his coming" (1 John 2:28). The witness of our Christian character shows a lost world that we have found the most excellent way to live—in Christ. We are living letters, "known and read by everyone" (2 Corinthians 3:2). While we have the *found* gospels of Matthew, Mark, Luke, and John, every Christian is a *living* gospel of Jesus Christ.

What is the gospel according to you, that your family, friends, and co-workers read?

Hopeful Lives

Since Christ is coming again, we are a hopeful people, looking forward to the Day of God.

"The day of God" of which Peter speaks (2 Peter 3:11–13) is the day Jesus returns. This is also "the day of the Lord," about which we read throughout the Bible. What a glorious day that will be! The apostle Peter uses the phrase *look forward* or *looking forward* twice in that passage.

The Christian faith is a forward-looking faith. God's grace gives us reason to look forward to every day when we awaken. As the psalmist proclaimed, "This is the day the LORD has made; we will rejoice and be glad in it" (Psalm 118:24 NKJV). We also look forward to the day of the Lord—the hope of humanity, the return of Christ.

Hope means a confident expectation based on the promises of God. Just as a car needs fuel to run, hope is the fuel of our faith. "Faith is confidence in what we hope for and assurance about what we do not see" (Hebrews 11:1). Hope is the hallmark of the Christian faith, fueled by the promises of God. Since we have the blessed hope of Christ's return, we live in the victory of faith over the fears of this life and faith in the life to come. "Everyone born of God overcomes the world. This is the victory that has overcome the world, even our faith" (1 John 5:4).

We are born of God the moment we trust in Jesus as our Savior and Lord. "To all who did receive him [Jesus], to those who believed in his name, he gave the right to become children of God—children born not of natural descent . . . but born of God" (John 1:12–13).

The Christian faith is a positive faith in a negative world.

Hurried Lives

Finally, since Christ is coming again, we are to live hurried lives. Peter tells us that we "ought to live holy and godly lives as [we] look forward to the day of God and speed its coming" (2 Peter 3:11–12).

Can we speed up the day Jesus will return? No, Jesus told us that no one knows "the times or dates the Father has set by his own authority" (Acts 1:7). But we speed the Day of God when we work with haste. Jesus said, "As long as it is day, we must do the works of him [God] who sent me. Night is coming, when no one can work" (John 9:4).

Personally I am always in a hurry. I like to move fast in life and keep on moving. Jesus wants us to speed up our pace as we share His good news of eternal life with our families, friends, and world. We need to take Jesus' challenge seriously: "As the Father has sent me, I am sending you" (John 20:21). If you are a slow mover, you need to pick up the pace in pursuing your life goals. Work hard and work fast and you will achieve more than others do.

My pastor told a story in a sermon that made a great impact on me as a teenager. After World War II ended, after the relentless bombing of the Nazis, Europe started the rebuilding process. Countless numbers of orphaned children lived on the streets of the cities that had been bombed to pieces.

One cold, foggy morning in winter, an American soldier in London was driving to his barracks. As he turned the corner in his jeep, he saw a little boy staring into the window of a bakery, where the baker was preparing the dough for a fresh batch of doughnuts. The aroma of the bakery filled the air.

The soldier pulled his jeep up to the curb and walked over to boy. The baker was removing the piping hot doughnuts from the fryer and placing them onto the glass-enclosed display for everyone to see.

The soldier asked the boy, "Son, would you like to have some of those doughnuts?"

The boy replied, "I sure would!"

The soldier went into the bakery, bought a dozen, and went back outside into the foggy cold. He handed them to the boy, smiling, and said, "These are for you." Then he started to get back into his jeep, when he felt a tug on his sleeve.

"Mister," said the boy, "are you God?"

"No," he replied. "But you could say I'm one of His children."

Takeaway

One day a man showed me the notes he had taken of my sermon. "I like your sermons," he said, "because they have take-home value." He used the sermon notes, he said, for motivational talks to his employees.

So let me conclude by giving you three take-home points for your life, as you consider Bible prophecy and the promise of Jesus' return.

First, *the world is safe in God's hands*. Bible prophecy reassures us that God is in control and that He is guiding the world to fulfill His purpose. Human chaos is held in check by divine control. I reiterate my point: The world is safe in His hands.

Second, *the will of God will be accomplished*. God "works out everything in conformity with the purpose of his will" (Ephesians 1:11). The pandemic will pass. Politics will settle down. Panic will subside. God's purposes will prevail. He is working out everything!

Finally, *the Word of God can be trusted*. All the prophetic signs Jesus gave that are being fulfilled in our time assure us that His Word can be trusted. His predictions and promises are true. Just as you can trust God's prophetic Word, you can trust His personal word to you. If you listen to the voice of the world, you will panic. If you listen to God, you will be at peace. So don't panic over politics or the world situation. Focus your heart and mind on the promises of God.

I read the following inspirational story many years ago and have often shared it to illustrate the hope God's Word gives us as we face life's challenges.

At the end of World War II, government representatives were sent to inspect the quality of childcare for youngsters whose parents had died in the war and who had been displaced by the Nazi invasion. They found that some children were at peace while others were terrified and traumatized.

In one home where an elderly couple were caring for some children, government officials saw how peaceful the children were. They asked the couple why the kids were so peaceful.

"First of all," they replied, "we love them as if they were our own children. Second, every night when we put them to bed, we place a piece of bread in their hands to clutch through the night, and we tell them, 'Don't worry, everything will be okay tomorrow.'"

That is what Bible prophecy means. God puts His Word of prophecy in our hands and says, "Don't worry—everything will be okay tomorrow."

ACKNOWLEDGMENTS

I want to thank everyone who worked so diligently with me on the book *Armageddon Approaching*. While world events can seem frightening and uncertain at times, Bible prophecy gives us hope that God is in control, and He has prepared a fantastic future for us.

I want to thank my wife, Barbie, an excellent minister in her own right, for her diligent proofing and editorial insights. I want to commend my executive assistant, Tracy Polson, for her invaluable input, editing, and administrative oversight of the manuscript. I also want to thank my media assistant, Sebastian Valderrama, for his editorial work and creativity.

I want to express my deep appreciation to Kim Bangs, editorial director of Chosen, for the opportunity to write the book and for her vision to provide a Christian resource that portrays the positive side of Bible prophecy to comfort and encourage the people of God. I want to commend the thoughtful and meticulous editorial work of Jane Campbell, who ensured the highest standard of excellence of the final

Acknowledgments

manuscript. She is the best editor with whom I have been privileged to work.

I want to acknowledge my close friend, pastor, and author Joe Dobbins for recommending me as an author. I also appreciate my good friend, author, and pastor Jentezen Franklin for the excellent foreword he provided. I appreciate all my friends and ministers who provided their endorsements for the book. Their support means the world to me.

I want to commend the entire team at Chosen Books for their vision, encouragement, and diligence to provide a much-needed resource to understanding the future according to our faith in Christ. Finally I want to thank the Mount Paran Church family for their personal support and partnership in ministry as we work together to give the world hope in Christ.

NOTES

Introduction

1. Billy Graham, *World Aflame* (Doubleday, 1965), 249.
2. "What Worries the World—August 2024," Ipsos, August 27, 2024, https://www.ipsos.com/en-nl/what-worries-world-august-2024.

Chapter 1 Prophetic Signs

1. Charles Gulston, *Jerusalem: The Tragedy and the Triumph* (Zondervan, 1978), 174–175.
2. "Islamic State: Egyptian Christians Held in Libya 'Killed,'" BBC News, February 15, 2015, www.bbc.com https://www.bbc.com/news/world-31481797.

Chapter 2 Future Shock

1. Alvin Toffler and Adelaide Farrell, *Future Shock* (Random House, 1970).
2. Strong's Lexicon, "G5568 – psalmos," Blue Letter Bible, accessed January 22, 2025, https://www.blueletterbible.org/lexicon/g5568/kjv/tr/0-1/.
3. Jun-Youb Lee, "The History of God at Harvard," *The Harvard Crimson*, January 28, 2020, https://api.thecrimson.com/article/2020/1/28/lee-history-god-harvard/.
4. Lee, "History of God at Harvard."
5. "Shield and 'Veritas' History," Harvard Graduate School Christian Fellowship, accessed January 22, 2025, https://hgscf.org/harvard-shield/.

Notes

Chapter 3 Israel Under Siege

1. Gulston, *Jerusalem*, 226.
2. Gulston, *Jerusalem*, 226.
3. Eliahu Elath and William L. Ochsenwald, "Israel," Britannica, November 21, 2024, https://www.britannica.com/place/Israel/Climate; and "Jewish Population Rises to 15.7 Million Worldwide in 2023," The Jewish Agency for Israel, September 15, 2023, https://www.jewishagency.org/jewish-population-rises-to-15-7-million-worldwide-in-2023/.

Chapter 4 The Days of Noah Return

1. Warren E. Leary, "Found: Possible Pre-Flood Artifacts," *New York Times*, September 13, 2000, https://www.nytimes.com/2000/09/13/world/found-possible-pre-flood-artifacts.html.
2. Rhonda Moniz, "Dr. Robert Ballard May Have Proof of Noah's Flood," *Marine Technology News*, December 28, 2012, https://www.marinetechnologynews.com/blogs/dr-robert-ballard-may-have-proof-of-noahe28099s-flood-700322.
3. "Sinews of Peace, 1946," America's National Churchill Museum, accessed January 22, 2025, https://www.nationalchurchillmuseum.org/sinews-of-peace-iron-curtain-speech.html.
4. Edgar A. Guest, "I'd Rather See a Sermon than Hear One Any Day," *The Passing Throng* (Portable Poetry, January 1, 2020), Kindle.

Chapter 5 The Society of Sodom

1. J. Yeargin, "The Midnight Cry," SermonCentral, November 28, 2006, https://www.sermoncentral.com/sermons/the-midnight-cry-j-yeargin-sermon-on-second-coming-98761.
2. Yeargin, "The Midnight Cry."
3. William Barclay, *The Gospel of Matthew*, 3rd ed., *The New Daily Study Bible* (Saint Andrew Press, 2001).
4. Clovis G. Chappell, *Feminine Faces* (Abingdon, 1942), 21.
5. Hy Pickering, *Twice-Born Men: True Conversion Records of 100 Well-Known Men in All Ranks of Life* (Pickering and Inglis, 1932), 137–139.

Chapter 6 The Coming Global Order

1. Bertrand Russell, *Icarus or The Future of Science* (New York: Dancing Unicorn Books, 2021), 19.
2. "The 2024 World Watch List," Open Doors, accessed November 18, 2024, https://www.opendoorsus.org/en-US/persecution/countries/.

Notes

3. *The Great Divorce* by CS Lewis © copyright 1946 CS Lewis Pte Ltd. Extract used with permission.

4. Told by D. James Kennedy, "The Spiritual State of the Union '93," Coral Ridge Ministries, https://www.djameskennedy.org/video-detail /2102os-the-spiritual-state-of-the-union.

Chapter 7 Antichrist Arising

1. *Surprised by Joy* by CS Lewis © copyright 1955 CS Lewis Pte Ltd. Extract used with permission.

Chapter 8 The Power behind the Throne

1. *The Screwtape Letters* by CS Lewis © copyright 1942 CS Lewis Pte Ltd. Extract used with permission.

2. Mike Mariana, "American Exorcism," *The Atlantic,* December 2018, https://www.theatlantic.com/magazine/archive/2018/12/catholic -exorcisms-on-the-rise/573943/.

3. Katie Jagel, "Half of Americans Believe in Possession by the Devil," YouGov, September 17, 2013, https://today.yougov.com/society/articles /7266-half-americans-believe-possession-devil.

4. Christina Zhao, "Video: Parkland Shooter Nikolas Cruz Punches Own Face, Says He Hears Demons in Confession Tapes," *Newsweek,* August 9, 2018, https://www.newsweek.com/parkland-shooter-nikolas -cruz-punches-own-head-says-he-hears-demons-1065071.

5. Jada Rivera, "Know Your Enemy," Proceedings, U.S. Naval Institute, March 2022, vol. 148, https://www.usni.org/magazines/proceedings/2022 /march/know-your-adversary.

6. *The House of Rothschild*, directed by Alfred Lloyd Werker (Twentieth Century Pictures / United Artists, 1934).

7. Paul E. Billheimer, *Destined for the Throne* (Bethany House, 1975), 17–18.

Chapter 9 The War to End All Wars

1. "We Came in Peace for All Mankind," NASA, last updated July 20, 2020, https://www.nasa.gov/image-article/we-came-peace-all-mankind/.

2. John F. Walvoord, *The Rapture Question* (Zondervan, 1979), 550–551.

Chapter 10 Global Warming

1. "What Is Climate Change?," NASA, last updated October 21, 2024, https://science.nasa.gov/climate-change/what-is-climate-change.

Notes

2. Norman Vincent Peale, "Thomas Edison's Glimpse of Heaven," *Guideposts*, accessed January 22, 2025, https://guideposts.org/daily-devotions/devotions-for-men/devotions-for-faith-prayer-devotions-for-men/thomas-edisons-glimpse-of-heaven/.

3. Fyodor Dostoyevsky, *The Brothers Karamazov* (1880). Although the quotation used here is widely attributed to Dostoyevsky, English translations of *The Brothers Karamazov* do not have this precise wording.

4. Dennis J. DeHaan, "Commandment 1—Worship Only God," *Our Daily Bread*, September 11, 1994, https://odb.org/1994/09/11/commandment-1worship-only-god.

5. Andrew Chaikin, "Who Took the Legendary Earthrise Photo from Apollo 8?," *Smithsonian*, January 2018, https://www.smithsonianmag.com/science-nature/who-took-legendary-earthrise-photo-apollo-8-180967505/.

6. Allyson Gross and Jenell Johnson, "The 'Earthrise' Image and the Impact of the Apollo 8 Mission," *Astronomy*, December 2023, https://www.astronomy.com/space-exploration/apollo-8s-moment-of-grace/.

7. "America on the Move," Eyewitness, The National Archives, accessed January 22, 2025, https://www.archives.gov/exhibits/eyewitness/html.php?section=25.

Chapter 11 The Government of God

1. Albert Einstein quoted in "Atomic Education Urged by Einstein: Scientist in Plea for $200,000 to Promote New Type of Essential Thinking," *New York Times*, May 25, 1946, https://www.nytimes.com/1946/05/25/archives/atomic-education-urged-by-einstein-scientist-in-plea-for-200000-to.html.

Chapter 12 A Skeptic's Guide to Faith

1. Ralph Waldo Emerson, "Sovereignty of Ethics," *Lectures and Biographical Sketches*, reprinted from *North American Review*, May 1878, Emerson Central, https://emersoncentral.com/texts/lectures-biographies/sovereignty-of-ethics/.

2. Fulton J. Sheen, *Treasure in Clay* (Doubleday, 1980; repr., Doubleday, 2008), 323, Kindle.

DR. DAVID COOPER serves as the lead pastor of Mount Paran Church of God in Atlanta, Georgia, with 12,000 members. The mission of the church is to give the world hope in Christ. He is a noted author, therapist, and recording musician.

He serves as adjunct instructor for Southeastern University, Richmont Graduate University, and other institutions on leadership, Christian counseling, preaching, and pastoral ministry. His lectures are featured as part of the Church of God ministerial training program for licensed and ordained ministers.

He holds a graduate degree in counseling from the University of Georgia and a doctoral degree from Erskine Seminary. He is a licensed professional counselor with the state of Georgia and a registered civil and domestic relations mediator in Georgia.

His books include *Destiny*, *Every Day with God* authored with his wife, Barbie, *Unfinished Business*, *World Religions and Jesus*, *Super Self*, *Seven Stepping Stones to Success*, *I'm Spiritual Not Religious*, *Get Well Soon*, and *Apocalypse: A New Look at the Revelation*.

His sermons and Bible studies are featured on the *Pastor David Cooper* podcast, YouTube, and other media platforms. His music is available on major music platforms. He is a featured speaker for churches, schools, businesses, and civic organizations.

CONNECT WITH DAVID:

- PastorDavidCooper
- PastorDavidCooper
- @PastorDavidCooper
- @RealDavidCooper
- @PastorDavidCooper
- @DrDavidCooper